The Other Brother

The Search for Simon Holmes à Court

*I dedicate this book to the
memory of both my father
and Julian Hampton,
a dear friend*

The Other Brother

The Search for Simon Holmes à Court

GEOFF ELLIOTT

Wild Dog Press

This edition first published in 2005 by:

Wild Dog Press
PO Box 1649
Highlands North 2037
South Africa

Phone: (011) 440 5255
Fax: (011) 440 3181

e-mail: wilddogp@iafrica.com

Originally published in Australia by Allen and Unwin, 2005

ISBN 1 91979 082 9

Typeset in 13/16 pt Granjon by Midland Typesetters, Maryborough
Printed by McPherson's Printing Group, Maryborough, Victoria

Contents

Foreword   vii

One
Missing, *May–June 1977*   3
The Okavango, *1970s*   10

Two
The early days, *1939–59*   23
Life in the bush, *1959–66*   33
Lost at sea, *1967*   40
The Cold War spy, *1967–69*   52
A Caribbean affair, *1970–72*   58
Diego Garcia, *1972*   76
Reunited, *1973–76*   86
The Big Five, *Christmas 1976*   95
Ethnée's quest, *1977*   105
The discovery, *1977–80*   125

Three
The journalist, *1995*   133
A town's silence, *August 1995*   145
The forest's tragic secret, *January 2000*   156
Daphne's lament   173
Epilogue: An old friend returns, *2004*   180
What happened to them?   182
Acknowledgments   190
Note on sources   193

Foreword

Recreating the mystery that has dogged one of Australia's most prominent families was no easy task. The events leading to Simon Holmes à Court's strange disappearance happened over thirty years ago in Africa. Aside from some old newspaper clippings about 'the missing sculptor from Botswana' published in South Africa at the time, there was little to go on.

It meant relying on personal accounts from friends and family and matching those up with the few facts that were consistent from newspaper reports several decades earlier. On the occasions where the narrative has chosen a version of events which is in dispute with another, it will be clear within the narrative itself. Scenes are recreated using the hundreds of hours of interviews that went into this book and the dialogue is based on these accounts.

At first I relied on the journalistic practice of attributing everything—conversations and scene setters—back to its source. Old habits die hard and the structure soon became unwieldy. Eventually, I broke the shackles and let the story tell itself. I hope I have struck the middle ground where this can stand as a piece of journalism but also a fast-paced mystery novel.

There are no fictional characters in this novel except one: me. Over the years it has taken me to get this down on paper I toyed with a narrative that jumped from third person to first as I tried to weave in my own journey to discover the truth. In the end, this kind of switch in voice jarred too much and I chose to create a nom de plume and stay in third person. His name is Mike Carter. That's the only licence I took. Everything that happened to Carter within these pages happened to me.

This search started in 1995 and it was not until the last few years, after travelling back to Africa, that everything finally fell into place. Some of the evidence pertaining to Simon's life and his final days and hours may come as a shock. But I could only ever present the facts—facts that have been buried for a long time—and let the players involved speak for themselves. Doubt remains about Simon's last days. No one can know exactly how events transpired and, in the end, the readers must judge for themselves on the evidence available.

I never met Simon Holmes à Court; I was only ten years old and on another continent when he disappeared. But I feel I got to know him quite well—an intriguing character and, as you will see, a courageous adventurer. My only wish is that, if he could, he would say this was a fair representation of his life.

Voyage of Simon

RUSSIAN FEDERATION

N

USA

NORTH
ATLANTIC
OCEAN

Tropic of Cancer

HAWAII

CAPE V

BARBADOS

NORTH
PACIFIC OCEAN

GALAPAGOS IS

SOLOMON IS

SANTA CRUZ
NEW HEBRIDES
FIJI   TONGA   TAHITI   MARQUESAS

BRAZIL

Tropic of Capricorn

AUSTRALIA

SOUTH
PACIFIC OCEAN

Holmes à Court

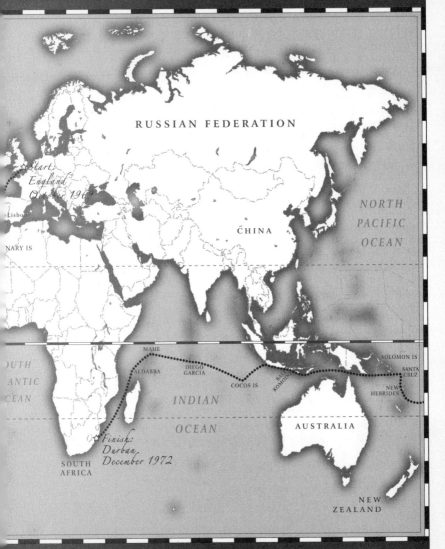

RUSSIAN FEDERATION

CHINA

NORTH
PACIFIC
OCEAN

Start:
England
October 1969

Lisbon

NARY IS

MAHE

ALDABRA   DIEGO
                 GARCIA

COCOS IS

                              BALI
                              KOMODO

SOLOMON IS

SANTA
CRUZ

NEW
HEBRIDES

OUTH
ANTIC
CEAN

INDIAN

OCEAN

Finish:
Durban
December 1972

SOUTH
AFRICA

AUSTRALIA

NEW
ZEALAND

One

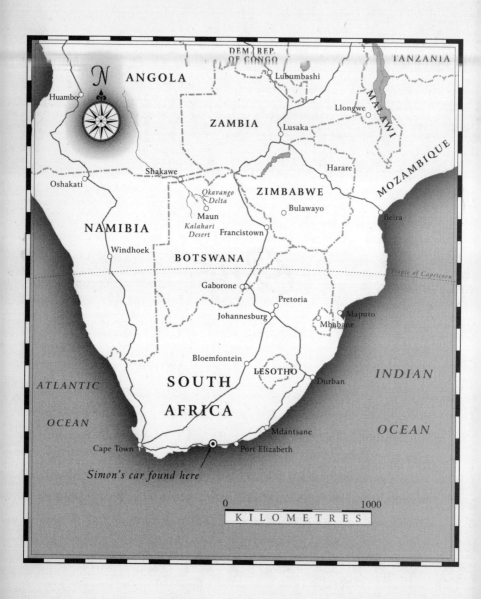

N

ANGOLA

Huambo

DEM. REP.
OF CONGO

Lubumbashi

TANZANIA

ZAMBIA

Llongwe

MALAWI

Lusaka

Oshakati

Shakawe

Harare

MOZAMBIQUE

NAMIBIA

Okavango
Delta

Maun

ZIMBABWE

Bulawayo

Beira

Kalahari
Desert

Francistown

Windhoek

BOTSWANA

Tropic of Capricorn

Gaborone

Pretoria

Johannesburg

Maputo

Mbabane

Bloemfontein

INDIAN

SOUTH

LESOTHO

Durban

ATLANTIC

AFRICA

OCEAN

OCEAN

Mdantsane

Cape Town

Port Elizabeth

Simon's car found here

0   1000

KILOMETRES

Missing

May–June 1977

Let him not be too moved when the birds of his land are singing, nor give too much of his heart to a mountain or a valley. For fear will rob him of all if he gives too much.
Cry, the Beloved Country, Alan Paton

On a wintry day in June 1977, Tsitsikamma forest workers took a little-used track down to the Vark River and stumbled across something odd. The workers could tell immediately it had been there for some time: a beige Datsun 620 pick-up with a back tray full of leaves and twigs. There were cobwebs in the wheel arches and across the doorjambs. They tested the doors; locked, as if the owner was always intent on returning. There were some belongings inside: a sleeping bag, some tools and two petrol cans. It was parked just off from a cleared part of the forest where people travelling down the highway might occasionally stop for a picnic, but the car had been successfully hidden from view, about two hundred metres from the main road.

The workers rarely saw strangers stop in the area. The lush and dank Tsitsikamma forest, nestled on the southern coast of South Africa about twelve hours drive east of Cape Town, is beautiful for its silence and loneliness. And, anyway, no one could remember seeing the vehicle before. Certainly, none of the bosses drove it around. And whoever left it there didn't want it found in a hurry, driven as it was into thick bush.

The workers were coloured folk—racial nomenclature still used in South Africa to this day—and part of an indentured workforce for the timber company in the area. They were dressed in striking orange and blue overalls, and they eyed their discovery curiously, testing the doors again and looking around the vehicle. They left to tell their supervisor. The tall yellow-wood trees surrounding the car stood guard, like silent sentinels keeping the secrets of a tranquil forest. Thick ferns and lush undergrowth grow quickly in this area and already the bush was doing its best to envelop the car.

The supervisors from the forestry station scrambled the police from the nearby Storm's River. When they arrived one enterprising sergeant managed to flick the driver's side lock and then hotwired the car. The engine turned over and he reversed it out of position and back into the clearing. The grasp of the creepers had to be torn away, as if they were reluctant to give up their prize.

The police immediately noticed something very odd. The numberplates had been jemmied off, and when they popped the bonnet the engine numbers had been bashed away, probably with a tyre lever. Clearly there was an attempt to conceal the identity of the vehicle and disguise any link with the owner.

Perhaps it was a professional hit on someone. Maybe there was a logical explanation for the missing numberplates and someone had simply parked their car there and gone camping. Brigadier Piet Hugo kicked around the bracken. He had made the trip to the area from Port Elizabeth, two hours by car, to check the scene himself. Brigadier Hugo was a divisional commissioner for the region and sensed there was something sinister behind this car and the state it was in. He was struck by the fact that this model Datsun could only be locked from the outside with the car keys. If it was a stolen and abandoned car, why would the thief bother to lock the vehicle afterwards?

He looked up at the Tsitsikamma ranges just over the valley—plenty of trekking trails up there and the little-used huts would make ideal cover for someone up to no good. It was a quiet time of year for tourists and the huts were rarely used.

'*Reël 'n toutrok* [someone organise a tow truck],' Hugo barked in Afrikaans. '*Ons sal hom terug sleep na die stasie op Stormsrivier en daar ondersoek* [we'll get it back to the station in Storm's River and do the forensics].' Still, he knew that unless something fell into their lap, the police investigation would take its time, especially since no one had been reported missing. He was hardly about to send out a search party. But his instincts told him it didn't look good, and a missing person was the last thing they needed.

The district was seething and the police force was kept busy trying to administer the hated pass laws, restricting blacks from travelling freely. Being an instrument of the apartheid machine of the day, divisional chiefs like Brigadier Hugo had a lot on their plate. He headed back to Port Elizabeth as the car was taken to the Storm's River police station, about eighteen kilometres away towards Port Elizabeth, down the N2 highway. There it would sit, and sit.

Weeks slipped by. Still the owner of the vehicle could not be established. No one had come forward saying his or her car had been stolen. Judging by the growth around the car when it was found on 9 June, the police estimated it had already been about a month since it was parked in the forest.

There were just a few police at Storm's River to pursue leads in the area, and no information was forthcoming. This was a sleepy hollow and usually the Afrikaner force handled domestic disputes among the impoverished coloured community working at the timber company. The workers, who were paid a pittance, drank away their wages in the company built villages, and only ever seemed capable of harming themselves. It was highly improbable any of them had a connection with the abandoned car.

The murder and robbery squad in Port Elizabeth kept the brief alive. Another team inspected the car at Storm's River and found something everyone had missed up until that point: an obscured metal plate pop-riveted under the bonnet with details of the car's engine number. Whoever had tried to conceal the identity of the vehicle had botched the job and left some clues.

Brigadier Hugo quickly reassembled his investigative team led by Major van der Merwe. The police called Datsun with the car's specifications and were surprised to hear it had come from Botswana, two days' drive to the north. It had been sold through a caryard in Francistown.

The car dealer was a local on-the-make tycoon, Arvi Farouk. Major van der Merwe telephoned Farouk. It was now mid-July, more than four weeks since the car had been found. Francistown was a small place and Farouk remembered the car and the owner. It was Simon Holmes à Court. The Afrikaner police stumbled over the name. Simon what? A double-barrelled name like that smacked of aristocracy. An Englishman? Afrikaners never had much time for Englishmen.

'Mr à Court,' the Major said, still struggling with the pronunciation and dropping 'Holmes', 'appears to be missing in the Tsitsikamma forest; his car has been found hidden in the bush.'

'What, on the coast of South Africa?' Farouk said. 'What the hell was he doing all the way down there?'

That's what the police wanted to know. Farouk explained that Simon was an adventurer and an experienced bushman. It was difficult to believe he would be stupid enough to get himself lost in a forest he did not know. A man well-versed in survival techniques who'd spent years in some of the harshest terrain in the world? 'He would never—'

'There has been an attempt to conceal the identity of the car,' the Major interrupted, adding gravely: 'The engine numbers have been bashed off, probably with a tyre lever.'

Farouk was shocked. 'Has he been murdered?'

'We have not yet found a body, but anything is possible.'

Farouk passed on the names and phone numbers of Bodo Muche and Tim Liversedge, two of Simon Holmes à Court's friends.

Muche, a sculptor and taxidermist, was running a company in Francistown called Botswana Game Industries (BGI). Liversedge was a budding photographer and naturalist who had been involved in the establishment of Botswana's wildlife and conservation department. Liversedge was living on the fringe of the Okavango Delta in a small town called Maun, about five hundred kilometres to the north-west of Francistown.

When Farouk hung up after speaking to the police he rushed over to BGI. Muche wasn't there. He spoke to company secretary Tom Burgess.

'Tell Bodo Simon's car has been found. It's in South Africa and the strange thing is the engine numbers have been bashed off to try to hide its identity. That's why it has taken them so long to contact us. I haven't seen Simon around since May. It doesn't look good, does it?'

Farouk hung up, and Tom Burgess went back to work, feeling a little anxious. A little later Muche walked into BGI's offices.

'Morning, Tom.'

'Bodo, something's wrong,' Burgess told him. 'The police in South Africa called Arvi. They've found Simon's car—in the Tsitsikamma forest. Someone has bashed the engine numbers off.'

Muche turned pale before Burgess's eyes, and slumped into his chair. His horrific nightmare came flooding back . . .

It was early morning on 6 May 1977, around the time of Simon's disappearance, when Bodo Muche jolted upright from a deeply unsettling dream. He was in a cold sweat and felt ill. An image of a rickety bridge in Maun was seared into his mind's eye. Muche could not shake the image. A tough, stocky East German, Muche had lived in Africa for more than twenty years. He was a no-nonsense character and not the type to be struck by premonitions—like a lot of hardened men and women who cut their teeth in Africa, Muche had long ago learnt not to dwell on things too much, you could go crazy otherwise. But his feeling that morning was that something awful had happened. The foreboding subsided over the next month until Burgess broke the news about Simon's car.

Burgess passed Muche a glass of water; he took it, hands shaking.

Muche told him how he had dreamt Simon was driving a grey Landrover and had crashed over the Matlapaneng Bridge in Maun, plunging into the Thamakalane River. Muche was suddenly there too, diving into the river to save him. But there was nothing, just darkness.

'I kept on diving again and again into this black hole. I kept seeing the pillars of the bridge whenever I came up for air.

'It was a very bad dream and I have just this lasting image of a bridge.'

The Okavango

1970s

The country was one intricate labyrinth of swamp, with many small streams moving outward from the river into the sandy wastes of the southwest. Where all this water goes is a mystery.

Aurel Schultz, explorer, 1897

Simon Holmes à Court was a powerful and fearless man hardened by a life of adventure and travel. He was 179 centimetres tall with sun-bleached brown hair and blue eyes. He was just thirty-seven when he disappeared.

For years he had been living in Maun, near the magical wetlands of the Okavango Delta in Botswana, modelling and sculpting animals. Maun (pronounced to rhyme with 'town') is an incredibly isolated, dusty frontier town—in summer the place is like a furnace, hardening its steely characters for the challenge of Africa. When the rains come things change, people relax, lose their inhibitions and the mischief begins. The wet season had just finished when Simon vanished.

It was so odd. Simon was beginning to feel settled after a life of wanderlust. But in early 1977 he had packed his Datsun with a few supplies and headed south on a rutted track to South Africa. It would be his last journey.

He drove into a political storm. South Africa was on the brink of civil war. This was the year that the disparate forces of South Africa's resistance started coalescing, a fact that worried the apartheid regime and would ultimately claim the life of Steve Biko, the natural leader of the resistance, just a few months later in September 1977. The last road Biko travelled before the police seized him was the N2 highway, winding its way along the dramatic coastline of south-east Africa and through the Tsitsikamma Coastal National Park. It was the last road for Simon Holmes à Court too.

Muche called his old friend Tim Liversedge in Maun to tell him the news. Bodo, Tim and Simon had all been good friends. Each was fiercely independent but also dependable.

Liversedge was deeply disturbed when he heard about Simon's disappearance, even more so when Muche told him about his dream. Muche was not the kind of man to exaggerate—he certainly wasn't flaky. Both men wondered why the hell Simon had travelled so far south. Liversedge told Muche Simon was headed to Johannesburg for supplies for a foundry he was setting up to cast bronzes.

Simon was capable of doing things out of the ordinary but they agreed this seemed really peculiar. Muche was also perplexed because Simon did not stop in at his house to stay the night; he was driving through Francistown, like he normally would on a trip south to Johannesburg.

Muche and Liversedge agreed that they should make contact with as many as possible of Simon's friends throughout the Okavango. Wildlife experts, artists, photographers and hunters, someone might know why Simon had headed south. Liversedge and Muche were sure, as the others would be, that Simon could not have met with foul play. He was too tough and too smart.

Liversedge frantically tried to establish Simon's movements in his final days and spoke with the South African police. They told him they had contacted all immigration points and discovered he had entered South Africa on Thursday 5 May at Kopfontein, a rarely used border post in the Western Transvaal, almost a day's drive from Maun. Ominously, it had been just a day before Muche's nightmare.

Liversedge found it hard trying to jog people's memories after so much time had lapsed and, anyway, a lot of the locals were busy travelling through the Delta. It was winter, the height of the tourist season in Maun, because winter is always dry and warm—just one of the contradictory forces at work which helped make the place so intriguing.

Simon had been living in a hut on the outskirts of town, on the banks of the Thamakalane at a place they called Croc Camp. He had a few friends, like Liversedge and Muche, but for the most part he kept to himself. He wasn't a boozer, steering clear of the reckless social life in Maun championed by the hunters, the focal point of which was Riley's Pub in the centre of town, a place for good times—and fights. Simon spent a lot of his days in the bush alone, which is why his lengthy absence did not raise any suspicions at first.

Maun was like that. There were just a hundred or so whites

living there while others would come and go over the years. Friends would not see each other for seasons on end and when they bumped into each other again, they would pick up conversations like they had only chatted yesterday. But news of the car being found so far away worried everyone. Over the next few weeks, Liversedge told all concerned 'He went to South Africa to obtain materials for the foundry, as far as I know, but from the day he crossed the border he hasn't been seen again.' When bumping into each other in the street, or at the pub, people tried to make sense of Simon's strange disappearance.

Jack Bousfield was one of the many legendary crocodile hunters of Africa in the fifties who had made a small fortune killing crocs for their skins in Tanzania. He eventually went into partnership with Muche in BGI, tapping the hunting-trophy market in Africa in the sixties and seventies, stuffing animals for well-heeled tourists. 'I'm sure I was the last one to see him driving out of town,' he told Liversedge one night at Riley's. 'He actually motioned for me to stop but I waved, pointing towards the petrol station and indicating I would come back.'

'I was only away ten minutes and when I returned he was gone.'

Bousfield was the last person in Botswana to see him alive.

It was such a jolt for the community. The mid-seventies in Botswana were the good times. The Delta brimmed with life, supporting an abundance of African wildlife like nowhere else on the continent and attracting a bunch of individuals with a common love for its incredible diversity.

In full flood the Delta is a giant swamp, bigger in area than the smaller countries of Europe. Most rivers flow to the sea, which makes an inland delta like the Okavango so unique. Maun starts to bake around August-September but that is when the water starts to flow. It is then that the rains which fall on the north-western Angolan highlands in the months before finally make their way down a meandering 900-kilometre stretch of the Okavango River to reach the neck of the Delta in Botswana. Crystal clear waters from the highlands sit atop what would otherwise be a desert floor. The Okavango River is a fat silver python snaking its way towards the Kalahari Desert and feeding one of the largest inland deltas in the world. A lattice of water channels spreads out over 22 000 square kilometres. The waters course their way over a horizon of papyrus beds and reeds, through channels and around small islands of palm trees, to eventually make it to Maun, to the south-east, about 250 kilometres from the head of the Delta.

Eventually, the full force of the Angolan floods peters out in the parched sands of the Kalahari. Without this regular flush of water through the town, Maun would risk becoming another sand dune. Instead, a magical river, the Thamakalane, fed the town folk; a river pregnant with bream and echoing to the melodic cries of the fish eagle.

Maun had started attracting an eclectic bunch of whites in the decades before. The first generation were mostly hunters, characters around whom author Wilbur Smith—a regular visitor to the Delta—centred so many of his African tales. Then the anthropologists and scientists came, feeding the grand institutions of science, such as the Smithsonian, with their research on the wildlife, the Bushmen, the Kalahari and the Delta. Maun was pegged as a frontier town for white establishment, in cohabitation with the indigenous peoples, the Batawana, the Bushmen and the Herero.

The sight of the proud Herero women offered a startling contradiction in Maun. The Herero were not dressed in the rich colourful fabrics of Africa—they wore Victorian-era style dress, with large bonnets and bustling skirts and cloaks. The skirts were ankle-length and the blouses came to their wrists—it didn't matter if it was 40 degrees Centigrade outdoors, each day the women would dress this way, in reds, greens and blues, like they were headed to a Victorian-era pageant.

The Herero are a pastoral people who are thought to have migrated from central Africa and settled around the Kalahari and further west in Namibia in the 1600s. Late in the nineteenth century, as Europe embarked on its scramble for Africa, these people became subject to German colonial influence and inherited the dress sense. It's their only remaining attachment to Germany.

Like with other colonial powers and their subjects, the Herero were soon in bitter land disputes over grazing in what was then known as South West Africa. Land had been given to German settlers and the Hereros wanted it back, mounting a violent campaign to reclaim it, killing one hundred and fifty German settlers in 1904. The German response was rapid, waging a war of extermination against the Herero. Many ran from their land and found their way north-east to the Kalahari and as far afield as Maun. The women, however, kept the Victorian dress tradition alive. They would gather on the streets of Maun, chatting in groups and looking as though they were taking a tea break from a shoot on a film set, so out of place was the dress code.

Delta men like Simon only ever wore khaki shorts, shirts and sandals or *veldskoene* (soft felt boots). As one of about a hundred or so whites who, by the seventies, had made their home in Maun, he lived alongside the thousand or so indigenous peoples. When it came to race, everyone seemed to get along okay.

But as in any small community, there was a certain level of tension caused by living in close quarters in conditions that were sometimes oppressive. This could erupt hilariously, as happened with the eccentric chap working in the wildlife department who had heard about the introduction of 'speed traps' in the big cities. He had grown tired of drunken Maunites running over his chickens as they sped away from the infamous Riley's Pub in the town's centre, so he decided to dig a deep trench to 'catch' the cars. One night a drunk sped down the road, a dozen people perched in the back tray of his four-wheel drive. The car plunged into the trench and they all went flying. No one was seriously hurt but the car was a write-off. There were the darker moments, though. On one occasion the wife of a well-known identity walked into the centre of town with a loaded shotgun demanding to know where her husband was, determined to shoot him for his indiscriminate affairs. She was wrestled to the ground.

Maun was so far away from anywhere. Even the magic of the Delta, its animals and its wetlands, was often not enough to lift the spirits of the whites. There was the crushing boredom of the same seasons and the same people; the same small-town problems, again and again. There was no tarred road out of Maun, and it was a day's drive through the desert and saltpans to the nearest town for supplies.

In many ways it was a spoilt existence; the whites were able to employ the Batawana to do their chores and keep their houses clean while they pursued their dreams on the Delta: hunting, science, filming or building exclusive tourist camps for A-list celebrities. But it meant they still had a lot of time on their hands. The men and women of Maun hit the bottle hard, and to relieve the boredom they would think nothing of risking life and limb for a 'jol' (a bit of fun)—like crocodile catching, for instance. Using a boat they would sidle up to a two-metre crocodile drifting down the river and then leap onto its back. Others would tape up its jaws and sling it into the boat. Invariably the thing would end up in someone's bed.

And there were so many affairs. During school holidays, when children returned from boarding schools in the south, there would be a mad scramble as their parents moved back to their matrimonial homes after living quite openly with someone else—it was all for the children's sake, of course. With all this white mischief, people sometimes got hurt.

It was a place without rules and regulations, in a time when scores were settled quickly. For all its problems Simon loved Maun and its adventurous folk. He kept returning there during a life of searching. He said the Delta was magical, calling it one of the greatest natural wonders of the world. And given the places he had seen, it was said with some authority.

There are many ways to meet one's maker in Africa. A first-time visitor is struck by it. If traditional African maladies like malaria don't get you, the snakes, lions, hippopotamus or buffalo will (now augmented by more modern curses like car crashes and AIDS). You can take care, of course, but it still means most Africans conduct their life as though every day is their last. Fate is a powerful concept in Africa and as much as modernity has tamed some of the continent's diseases and animals over the centuries, it still offers a fairly unsentimental and brutal view of the world in which the strong take all and the meek get nothing.

This is where it all began, the heart of Gondwanaland and the resting place of the world's earliest human inhabitants. Die in the African continent and you have the chance to close the circle on your evolution. Maybe it's why Africans, black and white, seem to accept that predatory forces of all kinds will often swoop to take away loved ones. That acceptance is a great challenge for any outsider living in Africa. There lies the great secret of this incredible continent: if you overcome your fear of death you overcome your fears in life and thus are liberated; you never look back; you keep moving.

Like a lot of people in the Okavango Delta, Simon cherished, and drew inspiration from, the environment in which he lived. But while some found their solace in a bottle, in beery companionship with their mates, Simon was a rugged individualist. He didn't care to socialise much with the hunters and steered clear of the booze and, for the most part, the marital shenanigans.

He never telegraphed his movements, which meant the few friends who were close to him knew that finding him after he disappeared would prove difficult. Southern Africa was an easy place to hide if you were on the run. It was becoming infamous for it. At the time Maun was awash with rumours that Lord Lucan, the aristocrat who apparently fled England in 1974 after allegedly killing his children's nanny, was holed up somewhere in the Delta—the rumours persist, although he's never been found.

Simon had headed to the southern forests of the Tsitsikamma alone. His family, living across the Indian Ocean in Perth, had no idea he was missing. Simon's brother Robert, who was carving out a successful business career, and Simon's mother, Ethnée, were used to not hearing from Simon for months on end. When news finally reached them of the bizarre way in which Simon's car had been abandoned, Ethnée was inconsolable.

Simon's adventurous life had been controversial at times. He had a habit of getting himself into, and out of, sticky situations, having broken all the rules. It was something he had been doing since his school days.

Two

The Early Days

1939–59

Oh! Mystery of man, from what a depth
Proceed thy honours. I am lost, but see
In simple childhood something of the base
On which thy greatness stands

                    The Prelude, William Wordsworth

Simon was a sensitive boy, unlike his more aloof brother Robert. They had a difficult upbringing, isolated from their parents in strict boys' boarding schools in South Africa from the age of eight in Robert's case, and seven in Simon's. It meant they grew to be tough and independent, but vulnerable too.

Mother Ethnée was 'born of the earth of Africa', as she liked to describe it, in 1915. She lived life like many of the privileged white children in Africa early in the twentieth century—indeed, like Victorian England used to be for the rich in the nineteenth century: surrounded by manicured lawns and servants. Ethnée never knew her father. Her mother

Florence left a troubled marriage when Ethnée was about two years old. Florence and Ethnée moved to Florence's parental home in a small country town called Somerset East in the Eastern Cape of South Africa in 1917. Ethnée would spend the next eight years there in a cosy and, by her own admission, spoilt childhood with mother, her grandparents and her aunt.

A wealthy farmer by the name of Harry Cummings courted Florence. He was twenty-two years her senior and they eventually married. Cummings' wealth was really the starting point for the riches that the Holmes à Courts would become famous for in Australia—Ethnée was never short of cash and it allowed her to put her children through exclusive schools.

Cummings was from Southern Rhodesia, now Zimbabwe. Florence and Ethnée relocated to his farm and Cummings, affectionately known as the Old Man, set about changing his young stepdaughter from something of a spoilt brat to a tough and independent young woman. As it happened, Ethnée grew to be a person of sharp wit and low tolerance for fools— a powerful individual in a small package. She measured only five foot or 152 centimetres. She studied at art school in Johannesburg in the 1930s and when she wasn't doing that she headed to the stables to go riding—her life on the farm meant she grew up to be an accomplished equestrienne. Ethnée loved horses. It was when she was out riding one day that she encountered Peter Holmes à Court, riding with his brother Anthony. Peter, at six foot three, or 190 centimetres, towered over Ethnée. He was tall, dark and handsome. He swept her off her feet.

Peter Holmes à Court was a descendant of the first Baron of Heytesbury, the link to British peerage that Robert Holmes à Court would immortalise for his family. (He called his private family company Heytesbury, along with the horse stud at Keysbrook, about an hour's drive south of Perth.) Peter had headed to the colonies in search of fortune, having quit the Royal navy. He was working at the Johannesburg stock exchange when he met Ethnée. They married in Johannesburg, in October 1936.

Robert was born in South Africa on 27 July 1937. Simon, who arrived two years later, on 26 October 1939, was born in Rhodesia, where Peter and Ethnée had relocated, back near the Old Man, who gifted them a big property. He also helped them buy a newsagency business in Gwelo.

Simon's birth was disastrous for Ethnée. She only just survived his delivery. He was born prematurely and Ethnée suffered serious internal damage at the hands of an impatient doctor trying to hasten the birth so he could go on holidays, Ethnée would later learn. At first she tried to get on at home, not realising her condition, but she steadily deteriorated over the following weeks. Her worried mother took Ethnée and the children to Cape Town so Ethnée could recover by the 'sea air'. She saw a specialist in Cape Town and was admitted to hospital where she would spend the next few months. She was lucky to survive, while Simon missed out on those vital first few months with his mother, fed and cared for instead by his nanny and grandmother.

Ethnée recovered but, soon after, more heartache followed. Peter was called up for service in World War II. The war changed everything for the family—Peter would return a shattered man. He miraculously survived a bombing on the HMAS *Delhi* in the Mediterranean and convalesced in

England before eventually returning to Cape Town in 1944. He suffered migraines and nightmares—what would these days be called post traumatic stress disorder. The family came to meet him on his return and they spent fifteen months together in Cape Town. Ethnée had written off the new sagency business—soaring paper prices during the war bankrupted the business after just three years.

Robert and Simon were sent to the Lion Crest preparatory school, at the foot of the Lion Head's hill in the city's centre. Peter, battling his own demons, was stern with the boys and attempted to rub some tough lessons into his kids early— Robert, then seven, and Simon, five, were forced to catch buses to school without a chaperone. It was the sort of early lesson in independence that would become a character trait of the boys later in life.

Cape Town would be the only occasion the family spent any length of time together, sharing the port-side ambience of a city that has always had so much to offer. Ever since Portuguese explorer Bartholomeu Dias rounded the Cape of Good Hope, foreigners have been arriving in Cape Town enchanted by its physical beauty and the presence of the mighty Table Mountain.

The good times in Cape Town did not last. Peter and Ethnée headed back to Salisbury (now Harare) in 1945 and Robert was sent off to Cordwalles boarding school in Natal in the east of South Africa soon after at the age of eight. Simon spent a year in Salisbury with his parents before he too was sent to Cordwalles at age seven. Their parents were more than 1600 kilometres away and the boys would return home just twice a year.

Ethnée and Peter were determined to give their children the best education possible in South Africa, despite the heartache of being so far away from their sons. During this time, however, Peter's troubles only grew worse and the marriage suffered. He would eventually leave Ethnée for another woman, remarrying in 1952, when Simon was twelve and Robert fourteen. Ethnée was heartbroken and any sense of rejection the boys felt was likely to have been exacerbated when, on the rebound, Ethnée remarried, this time to a hard-drinking journalist named Ian McKenzie, who Robert and Simon couldn't stand. Almost as soon as she wed, Ethnée was preparing to divorce the man, saying his drinking was an embarrassment. It was a chapter in her life she would rather forget.

Peter Homes à Court died in 1966. Over the years Robert and Simon had had little to do with him. This turbulent parental dynamic, and being institutionalised in the boarding school system from an early age, surely accounts for the aloofness both Robert and Simon were noted for. There was an inability to communicate on a deeply personal level, only a fierce determination to rely on no one else but themselves. Simon, according to his friends, grew to be an incredibly shy and very sensitive adult. He seemed closer to his animals, like the pet python he called Claude, than to other people.

After Cordwalles, the boys had been sent to the exclusive Michaelhouse grammar school in Natal in South Africa, the equivalent of Eton in the UK or Geelong Grammar in Australia. Despite their similarities, schoolteachers noticed the stark differences between the two boys. Robert spoke of moneymaking ventures while Simon was always absorbed in nature, more interested in collecting snakes than collecting good scores.

Michaelhouse, when the Holmes à Court boys attended, was an archetypal public school with its strict student hierarchy, its fagging, its flogging, its bullying, and the parental wealth. The school had very rigid rules and there was a postwar authoritarianism about the place. Michaelhouse also had a formal prefect system in which only the prefects' closest friends called them by their first names. Anyone junior to a prefect could be punished for buck (cheekiness) if there was not an adequate degree of deference.

Young boys were trying to be young men. It was a place where juniors were not allowed in any circumstances to put their hands in their pockets. There were starched collars with studs and any slight indiscretion in dress was dealt with severely.

A day in the life of a boy at Michaelhouse in 1956 began with the 6 am bell, followed by a cold shower or the plunge pool—and in winter the temperatures are freezing in this area. There would be a roll call before 6.30 am and lessons through to 1.15 pm. Then it was lunch, then sport, with rugby the most important game. The boys would be in bed by nine. It was a harsh environment and the juniors were subjected to a lot of punishment by the senior boys. If your bed was untidy or you were a couple of minutes late for a lesson, it meant the cuts—usually a couple of cane strokes across the bum.

In this rigid system, Robert Holmes à Court stood out among the toffs thanks to personality alone—the signs already evident of how the man would build a $1 billion fortune in the eighties as he rode the speculative stockmarket boom.

Robert showed his early entrepreneurial bent by lining up his camera when all official school photos were taken and he'd take pictures either just ahead of or immediately after the official photographer, then sell them to the boys at a significantly reduced rate. He was an engaging salesman—and the masters encouraged this entrepreneurship by allowing him to sell the photos a week before the official photographer, along with special offers to encourage buyers.

Simon was different. While Robert was gregarious, forthcoming, popular and had a lot of friends, Simon was the shy and retiring loner. He was obsessed with nature, especially snakes. Of his school subjects he took a particular interest in biology, which was his best subject.

Sundays were spent off the school grounds and Simon would be out before anyone else at the earliest possible moment, headed for the remotest farms, often alone. He would come back with pillowslips filled with snakes and animal skeletons. He would then catch frogs to feed the snakes. If it had to do with nature, Simon was into it. The school rule forbade him catching poisonous snakes but he went ahead and did it anyway—catching mainly puff adders by hand.

While a lot of Simon's friends were into classic literature—like Hugh Roberton, who would go on to become a successful political journalist in South Africa—Simon would be engrossed in accounts of expeditions to remote places. While Roberton and his poet wannabes would sit atop a hill with a wind-up gramophone, blasting the countryside with Beethoven, Simon would be in the bush fossicking for snakes.

One of the unwritten rules at Michaelhouse was the requirement to hike to Inhlazane, Zulu for 'maiden's breast' and referring to a mountain twenty-three kilometres from Michaelhouse. While many found once was enough, Simon had done it four or five times.

'He joined our group on the hike, and people felt safe with Simon,' Roberton said. 'We left at 3 am, hiked to the top and scratched our names in the beacon there. One incident during that trek was coming across a cobra, which reared up in the path. There were about six of us: we had to stop while Simon made an attempt to catch this thing and we were all relieved just to catch our breath: Simon had set a blistering pace. I was aware that on these journeys he was a different person, much happier. While those treks were something to be endured by most of us, Simon loved it.'

Simon also caught the attention of the schoolmasters, all of whom hailed from the English public school system. Robert and Simon were in Tathan house and the housemaster, Ronald Brooks, despaired of Simon's 'complete recklessness, utterly fearless behaviour. He was the daredevil adventurer sort of chap; not too fond of school work.' It seemed Simon was always in some kind of trouble at school usually thanks to his determination to collect snakes and other reptiles and bring them back to school, whereas Robert was more serious about his academic school life.

'Robert had a sort of reserve and dignity about him, a very sure sort of person. But the two of them had quite a reputation with staff as being pretty wild. Even Robert,' Brooks said.

On one occasion at the beginning of 1956, Robert flew into school behind the wheel of a car, with three other Rhodesian boys, including Simon, as passengers. It was unheard of that any schoolboy would drive a car to school. Robert went to the rector and said: 'Instead of coming by train I brought these chaps down and charged them what would have been the rail fare. I am eighteen; all I ask is that I be able to leave the car here, not use it during term, and take them back at the end of term.' There was a full housemasters' meeting to discuss this completely new venture. Back and forth they debated the ethics of giving responsibility to one boy to cart other schoolboys around. But in the end Robert pulled it off. A strong personality and confidence meant he was able to negotiate with the authorities, something the other boys wouldn't dare have done.

Simon lived in this shadow. He was very fond of Robert at school, his friends and housemasters said, and there was clearly a bond between them. But Robert was a prefect in later years and kept his distance. And at this early age Simon appeared to draw support and inspiration from his fearless interaction with Africa's wildlife. Robert, after a few false starts after leaving school—including a restaurant in Cape Town—would emigrate to Australia in his mid-twenties, read law, and make the Holmes à Court name famous. The press would come to call him the Great Acquirer, a man who rode the 1980s asset boom and became Australia's first billionaire.

While Robert was charting a spectacular corporate career, his little-known brother was most likely out in the Okavango Delta, keeping an eye on poachers. He eschewed city life and on leaving school went bush, meeting up with a family friend, Patrick Bromfield, who was the first, and at that time the only, game ranger employed by the embryonic wildlife department. He was based in Francistown in the Bechuanaland Protectorate, as Botswana was known then. In 1959 Simon started training as a game warden. He was nineteen. The civil service rules stipulated that no one could be employed under the age of twenty-one, but Simon was so determined he worked for nothing those first two years. His dedication meant that as soon as he came of age, he formally applied and the job of game warden was his.

Bechuanaland was a British territory, but like elsewhere in Africa, independence movements were gathering momentum. Francistown, as the administrative capital, was well known as a listening post for the various insurgencies around sub-Saharan Africa. The place was full of spies—something that would later come to haunt Simon. But for now he was doing what he had always wanted to do—spending days on end out in Africa's magical wilderness.

Life in the Bush

1959–66

My fate cries out,
And makes each petty artery in this body
As hardy as the Nemean lion's nerve.

Hamlet, William Shakespeare

Simon lived in a simple second floor apartment in government-sponsored accommodation in Francistown. He would live there from 1960 until 1967. His life meant long periods in the bush, leading local black game scouts around the fringes of the Delta, not only monitoring the hunters but culling animals as well, in accordance with the brief at the time to protect Botswana's nascent agricultural industry. On occasion Simon was forced to shoot rogue elephants that were damaging crops—something he hated to do. He once walked for days on end, alone, through the African bush, driving a herd of elephants away from some crops when his brief had been to shoot them. He told his mother he never wanted to shoot another elephant in his life and would do anything to protect them.

Life as a game warden was an ideal vocation for a man like Simon. People would say Simon had a sixth sense—an ability to communicate with animals on some level. He was probably the most respected man in the Delta for his stamina and completely fearless approach. He would walk for days and days with just a packet of mealie meal—cornmeal—tracking animals and hunters. He had an almost mystical ability to creep up on the hunters in the middle of the bush without anyone noticing. He could even take the well-attuned black scouts by surprise. Hunters would always be looking over their shoulder because they knew Simon was out there somewhere, watching.

In this way he kept a check on the hunters to make sure they stayed in licensed hunting areas. He was always on foot, walking twenty kilometres or more in a day, camping rough under Africa's stars in an area boasting more lions than most other areas of Africa. He was like that, friends would say, immune to the danger. Indigenous Africans were astounded at his ability to move at ease among the predators and the giants.

Simon knew how to stare down a beast too.

Show fear, thought Simon, and I'm dead. There was only one thing to do: he drew a deep breath between clenched teeth and rose from his crouch.

Arms raised and screaming at the top of his lungs, Simon charged the elephant. It was a massive bull. About thirty years old,

Simon reckoned. One tusk was straighter than the other—many of the perfect pairs having been poached in recent years—but both were brilliant white against a grey and ochre backdrop. The bull had just caught Simon's scent but he was using the moments of surprise in his favour. Just as the bull was about to fan its ears like massive bellows, Simon charged. What a fright! The noise and a spectacular display of aggression: the elephant backed up, trumpeted and moved off behind the acacias.

'Shoo, go on, shoo. Get out of here! Go on, move it,' yelled Simon. The bull backed up still further and trotted off, trumpeting hesitantly: confused, no doubt, that such a gnat had called its bluff.

Simon smirked and dusted off the water bottle he had hurled at the beast. He had been wandering through the Delta for two days now, and there had been a few close shaves: he almost stumbled into a lone buffalo as it lay in a gully; and a pride of lions had decided to spend last night sleeping next to his tent. Then he had skirted too close to this bull. Normally it would be okay, so perhaps this chap had been shot at before and was nervous, flighty. Charging a bull elephant—for audacity it was probably Simon's best effort yet.

He was at his happiest out here in the Delta, alone and away from the boozy banter and bravado back in Maun. Tour hands and game rangers were always telling tourists stories about the danger—the near misses and horror stories of those fallen. But there would be no beery boasting in Maun that night. Simon kept to himself.

His fellow game rangers had tried to convince him to stay for the weekend—there was a big party going down—but Simon said he was off to the bush. So overt was the peer group pressure that one local hunter had decided to steal Simon's carburettor cap from his Datsun to keep him in town. It gave Simon a chuckle—he had been planning to set out on foot anyway.

As he left Maun one of the hunters tore around a corner on a dirt track in his battered Landrover. He had been at his safari camp but was heading back to Maun for the party.

'Where the hell are you going, Simon?'

'For a bush walk.'

'How long will you be gone? Just so we know when to send out the search party,' the hunter joked.

'Only a couple of days. I want to see how those tsetse traps are doing.'

'Man, you'll miss a helluva party. People coming from all over, down from Kasane and even Salisbury.'

'Oh well, have a good time.'

Simon pushed on. The hunter revved the Landy, pumped the clutch and crunched the rumbling, rattling motor into second gear (first gear went missing years ago) and chugged off. *Strange lad,* he muttered to himself, raising the bottle of warm beer to his bloated, stubble-covered face. Then he set his mind to the task ahead that night: bagging one of the 'big five'. It was a hunting expression, but it was something of a double entendre in town, all to do with a particular group of young women.

Spending weeks on end in the bush meant it was difficult to make friends. Simon's only deep friendship at this time was with Bodo Muche. They used to play chess and share a few quiet beers when Simon came back to town after a spell away. Muche made friends easily and his hospitality was legendary. People often stopped over at his place as they made their way down south to Johannesburg. He was infamous for having a sauna at his home. In those days the twenty-something men and women, in their prime, fit and tanned, would crowd Muche's sauna on a stopover. The afternoon get-togethers often dragged into lengthy all-night parties. Muche's sauna— a testimony to his central eastern European heritage of health spas, saunas and cold showers—is still talked about to this day by men in their sixties and seventies who get a glint in their eye every time it's mentioned.

Simon was something of a coy observer during these parties. He was always shy around women, a deeply secretive young man to whom few could get close. Over the years Muche broke through and, of anyone, was probably the closest to Simon.

But the British establishment was also closely watching his progress. Bromfield had links with the British at Mafeking, on the southern border of Botswana—a British bolthole since the days of the Anglo Boer War. Ethnée had even been invited to meet the High Commissioner of the protectorate in 1959 because, it seems, even after a few months on the job, and without pay, the Brits were impressed with Simon's self-reliance in the bush. This meeting in 1959 sparked a new adventure for Ethnée too.

In the late fifties Ethnée had met and fallen in love with Charles Trevor, a successful civil engineer in Rhodesia who ran his own engineering business in Salisbury, and they were planning to set up a new business together in the hospitality game. They had been thinking to locate it somewhere near the southern coast of South Africa, but at the meeting with the High Commissioner—with Bromfield acting as a broker—the possibility arose of a British tender to develop a new hotel on the Chobe River in northern Botswana. Bromfield had already started the park with Simon's help. The area was spectacular, with the wide river bordered by plentiful pasture and shaded by a canopy of trees. African game was ever present, from antelope and elephant to the big cats: lion and leopard. Ethnée and Charles were excited by the prospect and agreed to tender. Within a month they had won the concession and set about moving their belongings from Rhodesia to establish camp and start building a hotel.

It would be a five-star resort, even attracting the likes of Prince Bernhard of the Netherlands in 1963, who Simon chaperoned on safari in his position as head game warden. The prince was thrilled with Simon's knowledge and skill in finding animals to photograph. On his return to the Netherlands, the prince sent Simon a Rolex watch via diplomatic post—so he didn't have to pay any duty.

By all accounts Ethnée's Chobe lodge was a huge success, but tragedy struck the following year. In April 1964 Charles took two friends fishing on the Chobe. They were attacked by a swarm of bees. Charles was severely stung and all three were flown to hospital in Rhodesia from the makeshift airstrip Charles had carved out of the wilderness there. While the two friends—Yvonne and Petey from Cape Town—pulled through, Charles did not. For six weeks he hung on, Ethnée and Simon by his bedside in the hospital. But he had suffered massive internal damage from the bee poison and died. He and Ethnée had been together seven and a half years.

Understandably, the Chobe lodge lost its appeal for Ethnée after this tragedy. She set about selling it and arranged a trip to Australia to be reunited with Robert, now studying law in Perth. She stayed there for eight months, until September 1965, with Robert urging her to sell up in Africa and settle in Perth, saying the political climate in Africa would only get worse.

Things were changing in Africa. In 1966 the British acceded to independence for the Bechuanaland Protectorate and it marked the end of Simon's time as a game warden. The British ceded control to the newly named Botswana on 30 September 1966, a month before Simon's twenty-seventh birthday. Civil servants like Simon were given the choice to stay on or take a stipend, and Simon chose the latter: a British pension that, for a man of modest means like Simon, was enough to live on.

Simon's decision to leave the game department meant he was removed from playing a direct role in monitoring the hunters and the wildlife of the Delta. He told his mother at the time that if he wasn't going to be near the animals on land he might as well try exploring another world: the sea. Simon had dreams of pursuing a career in underwater photography as well as offering charter services and diving. This was no small ambition for a man from landlocked Botswana. Simon thought nothing of setting up a business with sailing as its core activity, despite not knowing the first thing about sailing or the dangerous seas around the southern tip of Africa and Madagascar, where he planned to take tour groups.

Simon was obviously blinded to any risks if he assumed he could set something up and get it running quickly. It would turn out to be a terrible mistake.

Lost at Sea

1967

'Wouldst thou'—so the helmsman answered—'Learn
the secret of the sea?'
Only those who brave its dangers
Comprehend its mystery.
The Secret of the Sea, Henry Wadsworth Longfellow

While Simon did not care much for trying to make millions of dollars, he was not immune to sibling rivalry—brother Robert was on the way to establishing his own law practice and making a killing trading on the share market. Robert had even taken his first company directorship at the age of twenty-nine in early 1967. Simon thought he too could make a success of running his own business and wrote to Robert asking him about the formation of partnerships. He planned to team up with an acquaintance, Julian Marshall, who had been working in the fishery department in the Bechuanaland Protectorate and had also taken the pension. They planned to buy a yacht, using the payout they received from the British government.

Ethnée also helped out. She had moved back to Salisbury but had taken Robert's advice and was planning to leave Africa for Perth, to be closer to Robert, who was starting a new family having married university sweetheart Janet Ranford. Ethnée was torn about leaving her second son and did what she could to help Simon make a success of his new venture. Ethnée scoured the newspapers for a suitable yacht for Simon and spotted an advertisement in the Rhodesian newspapers for the *Carina*, a 31-foot ketch, for sale for about 5000 rand. The boat was acquired in February 1967. Salisbury was about 440 kilometres from the coast but only 20 kilometres or so from Lake Chivero, or Lake McIlwaine as it was known then, which was a popular sailing club for the whites, who often spent weekends sailing, barbecuing and boozing on its shores.

Simon had the yacht freighted by road to Beira, a port town on the coast of Mozambique. He and Marshall set about the next task: learning how to sail. They had some help from local sailors but it was wing and a prayer stuff and they soon found themselves in trouble.

On one occasion they ran aground just short of safe harbour, losing their way after mist enveloped them, and then the engine failed when it clogged with sand as they tried to power out. Night fell with the *Carina*'s keel wedged on the bank and Simon and Marshall sheltered below deck, trying to sleep as the yacht was subjected to a terrible pounding by the waves. They were woken during the night when the ketch crashed over onto its starboard hull as the tide fell.

They dug out the next morning on the rising tide and finally pushed off the bank under sail. The *Carina*'s hull was not damaged and under a distinctive blue mainsail they made it back to harbour. But it was a brush with the sea that Marshall was not prepared for and when they finally made it to land he told Simon that the sailing life was not for him, and abandoned the nascent partnership. And if Marshall had been thinking it was an omen of things to come, he was right. Disaster would soon follow.

Simon spent the next few days trying to fix a badly damaged keel, which needed repair work done in Beira, about thirty kilometres away. He is said to have walked some miles towards Beira with the keel over his shoulder—he was a tough, nuggety man—before being picked up by Eve and Lloyd Barber. They were sailors too, and took Simon under their wing to teach him more about sailing.

Despite Marshall's departure, Simon was determined not to give up after this first embarrassment. The keel was fixed and reattached and, with the Barbers' help, Simon's confidence increased enough for him to eventually sail single-handedly into the Mozambique Channel. His mettle was soon tested as he sailed 220 kilometres south from Beira to the azure waters around the Bazaruto Archipelago in October 1967.

In an extraordinary coincidence, at the same time Tim Liversedge was spending a month on this remote island, researching mammals for the Smithsonian, the Washington-based scientific institute for whom the young Liversedge, a budding naturalist, had been working for some years. Simon and Liversedge had met around 1964 and became friends, united by their love of Botswana. Liversedge spent most of his time in Maun but, like Simon, would be alone in the bush for weeks on end. The two would often bump into each other in remote locations—though neither expected to meet this far afield.

A month earlier Liversedge had chartered a boat and made

the crossing from Mozambique to Bazaruto Island. He had a boatload of equipment and had not seen a soul except for the two locals living on the island, who would sell Liversedge palm wine and fresh fish as he went about his work. One day the *Carina* appeared in the distance, cruised in slowly and weighed anchor in a bay in front of Liversedge's camp. Liversedge was stunned to see Simon row across from his yacht. It would be a characteristic of Simon Holmes à Court's life—turning up in the most remote places unannounced, true to his spirit of wanderlust and desire to be exploring new territory.

The two men spent a blessed few days together. The Bazaruto Archipelago is one of the beauty spots of Africa. The brilliant white beaches up and down Mozambique front the warm waters of the Mozambique Channel, which bustles with sea life rivalling any of the world's great marine breeding grounds. There is the painted lobster, with its massive antennae and spidery legs attached to a vivid blue-green carapace, looking every bit like an extraterrestrial landing craft as it crawls its way across a brilliant white seafloor. Above them, white pointers glide and there are massive sea turtles, huge grouper and stingrays in amongst a kaleidoscope of tropical fish.

In the sixties the coast and the outlying islands from Beira to the Bazaruto Archipelago were about as raw and unspoilt as they ever were. Bazaruto briefly blipped onto the radar screen during World War II—war ships had cruised the area and it was in the azure bays of the archipelago that Nazi tankers had berthed to refuel the fleet. But over the years there had been little other activity around these waters, aside from ships making their way up and down the Mozambique Channel (so named because here the Indian Ocean separates

Mozambique from Madagascar, which at its closest point is about 420 kilometres away to the east).

Bazaruto itself is just seventeen kilometres or so offshore from Mozambique. It's now a national marine park and protected from fishing. Some say Bazaruto is one of the most beautiful unspoilt islands in the world—its frosty white sands and palm-fringed beaches are attracting tourists in their thousands.

Simon told Liversedge he had sailed out of Beira a couple of days before and had decided to head to Bazaruto for some diving. But his scant knowledge of sailing immediately caused him trouble again. 'Before I even left port I almost collided with a massive tanker!' he said. But he also mentioned how he had been practising his snorkelling and diving, and he was keen to show Liversedge just how accomplished he was.

Later that day the two snorkelled their way to the edge of a big reef and Simon pointed out to Liversedge a huge grouper, looking more a like small submarine lying in shallow water on the edge of the shelf. Simon had a spear gun and speared the grouper in the back of the head. The fish gave two flicks of its mighty tail and was off, with Simon in tow. Simon had become an excellent free diver and could go down twenty to thirty feet, even sitting on the ocean floor for an age while fish gathered around him.

Liversedge watched gobsmacked as the grouper and Simon disappeared into the deep blue. A minute later Simon came up, gasping for air but still with his spear, which he had managed to wrench out.

Later that evening over fresh fish and palm wine by the camp fire, Simon told Liversedge of his plans: that he would set up a tourist venture. He was going to sail into Durban and establish his base there, recruit a crew for the *Carina* and start chartering the yacht. Durban was a bigger market and had the potential for more tourists. Within a few days Liversedge bade him farewell as Simon sailed south about eight hundred kilometres to Lourenço Marques (now Maputo), in Mozambique. On 13 October 1967, he set off again, this time to Durban. But it appears he was ill-prepared, sailing without the necessary permissions. The next few days would change everything. His plan, and life, were soon in tatters.

With little sailing experience Simon was traversing one of the most notorious stretches of water in the world. Some fierce currents intersect at the southern end of the Mozambique Channel. This is the Wild Coast and sailors don't take it on lightly. Huge waves in the channel do not just splinter yachts— they snap tankers in half. The legendary tales of ninety-foot waves in this area are enough to make an experienced hand proceed cautiously, let alone a novice.

In October, the Wild Coast's ten-knot southerly currents rush headlong into severe northbound storms. And a steep continental shelf drops away from the east coast, so there are few islands and few safe natural ports in a storm. Sailors port-hop down the Wild Coast in a race against time to duck into a safe harbour before the next low pressure sweeps up the coast. But it's tricky because the ocean currents and a solid 35-knot north-wester speed sailors towards these storms, so timing is critical. The winds can reverse within minutes and start gusting at 180 kilometres an hour. Mix that with two of the world's most powerful ocean flows—the Agulhas and Benguela —converging, and sailors are often trapped in Mother Nature's vortex and never seen again.

The Agulhas is the second fastest current in all the world's oceans but it's far deadlier than the fastest, the Gulf Stream, thanks to the funnel effect as it branches off to sweep through the Mozambique Channel. It's a combination of conditions wryly dubbed the 'South African Welcome' and it was waiting to greet Simon Holmes à Court.

After nearly a thousand years of crossing the Indian Ocean, Arabs, Persians and the fifteenth-century Chinese Star Fleet had never navigated the Mozambique Channel. What chance did a lone sailor with little experience have?

He left Lourenço Marques on 13 October and was due in Durban two days later. By 24 October he still had not arrived.

The headlines that appeared in South African newspapers in 1967 were uncannily similar to those that would appear ten years later—a portent of things to come. Simon Holmes à Court, the game ranger from Botswana, had disappeared.

On 26 October 1967, Simon's twenty-eighth birthday, the *Eastern Province Herald* reported:

Plane aids in search for ketch

Shipping and aircraft, including a SAAF Dakota from Youngsfield, Cape Town, had by last night reported no sign of missing ketch *Carina*, due in Durban last week from Lourenço Marques.

The 31-foot ketch, sailed by Mr Simon Holmes à Court, a Botswana game ranger, was reported sighted for about two hours off Scottburgh, 40 miles south of Durban, on Tuesday afternoon, but she has not been seen since.

And next day the press reported:

Hopes for safety of lone yachtsman Mr Simon Holmes à Court are fading as an intensive search for missing ketch, *Carina*, entered [its] fourth day today without success.

Robert spoke to Ethnée and told her to expect the worst. Simon had been missing for ten days. Robert had given him up for dead, and you couldn't blame him given the history of the Mozambique Channel.

In Salisbury on 25 October, Ethnée told newspapers: 'I'm so worried that I am wondering whether I should fly to Durban and charter a plane to look for him.' And she highlighted Simon's lack of experience in the ocean, saying it was one of the first times Simon had sailed alone and 'it was difficult for one man to handle a 31-foot ketch at the best of times'.

Ethnée decided to make her mercy dash to try to assist in the search for her lost son. She flew via Johannesburg and landed in Durban on 27 October. Simon had captured the attention of the nation, with radio updates and front-page headlines thanks to the massive search underway. Ethnée was flooded with messages and prayers for her son. There was the sighting in Scottburgh, some 34 nautical miles—about 64 kilometres—south and it was a hopeful sign, but it also meant he had been blown way off course.

Simon was hardy and resourceful but knew he was doomed if he was not found soon. For days he had been drifting down the coast,

the Carina *shattered. The big blow had snapped her sail battens like toothpicks and the sails themselves now fluttered uselessly, like torn rags in the wind. He had ridden through the worst of the storm and mountainous seas to be faced now with a final hour in far less dramatic conditions. The sea was calm, but he was shrouded in a thick sea fog; a suffocating pale blanket.*

Now, nearly two weeks after leaving Mozambique, he was at the mercy of currents that seemed intent on sweeping him towards the infamous Cape of Storms where the Indian Ocean meets the Atlantic.

Simon prayed the fog would lift. He had no communications; his two-way wrecked in the storm. Only his AM radio was working and through the static he picked up the news bulletins that planes had been searching for him—but in the wrong place. He knew he was well south of Durban now, where the rescue effort was centred. And the persistent fog made it impossible for any passing vessels to see him.

The Carina's *small outboard had been useless. It could not compete with the ocean currents and fuel was now spent in a vain attempt to make landfall.*

Still, Simon slipped into a routine, each day trying to resew both the mainsail and aft sail, working below deck in the cockpit and out of the sun. Day after day he sewed them up only to curse his unprepared kit—the weak fibre he used was no good. The sails would rip again every time he hoisted them.

But he never panicked. Simon was rarely ruffled. There was that fateful acceptance of things, like only Africans (black or white) can know.

He was well conditioned thanks to the weeks he would spend alone out in the bush. He knew he could live a long time on little food and water. Over the nearly two weeks he had been at sea he had lived mostly on rice but now his supplies of water were running low. He might have been inexperienced but he knew to stick to carbohydrates—protein requires more water to digest than carbohydrates. Still, on a couple of occasions he caught some fish and ate it fresh and raw—while there was still some moisture in it.

Then, late in the day on October 27, Simon spied a huge tanker. The captain and crew of the French vessel, the Ville de Lyon, *had also seen him. The tanker marked his position—183 nautical miles south of Durban. The* Ville de Lyon *veered towards the stricken yacht. The crew threw out a rope ladder and Simon clambered up.*

Despite the ordeal the crew remarked how fresh and unscathed he still looked. But before he even had a chance to celebrate, rescue papers were thrust in front of him for his signature.

Now for the payback, thought Simon. This is going to cost me. The papers stated he had asked that the Carina *be taken in tow. Typical of marine insurance, it puts the burden of cost back onto the sailor, including any lost time for the tanker. 'How on earth am I going to pay for all this?' he thought.*

The radio stations and newspapers of the day heralded his survival and Ethnée's elation. 'A MOTHER'S JOY— MISSING SON IS SAFE' as one newspaper reported. Ethnée was pictured on the telephone and captioned the 'most relieved woman in South Africa'.

Ethnée rushed to the Durban docks, boarded the yacht *Snow Goose* and sailed out with the media to greet Simon the next day as the *Ville de Lyon* rounded the coast towards Durban. His mother threw her arms around her stunned son, who was amazed at all the attention. At a celebratory function at the Durban Yacht Club he explained how huge seas and strong winds had blown him off course. Exhausted from fighting the storms, at one stage Simon had fallen asleep at the tiller, which caused the *Carina* to jibe suddenly and the sails ripped.

He might have been happy to be alive but any joy was short-lived. The plan to use the *Carina* to charter tourists and divers around the Mozambique coast would now have to be put on hold as he tried to repair the boat and pay off the enormous bills he faced. On 30 October 1967 the *Evening Post* painted a bleak picture:

Sailor faces bills

Simon Holmes à Court, the 28-year-old yachtsman who was towed into harbour here at the weekend, faces a big problem.

When the French tanker, *Ville de Lyon*, spotted him drifting helplessly with broken sail slats and ripped sails, off the Transkei coast on Friday, he thought his troubles were over.

But they were just starting.

Now he is faced with huge bills for towing and loss of time to the vessel.

'Before they took my yacht in tow, I had to sign a document saying I had asked to be taken in tow,' said Simon last night. 'The captain was most apologetic but explained it was the rule of the owners.'

The Durban representatives of the *Ville de Lyon* were handling the matter and he would see them today. 'Until I see them I do not know what my plans for the future will be,' he said.

If he loses his yacht, the *Carina*, he will still persevere with his plans to cruise Mozambique waters doing diving and underwater photography. 'This was my reason for sailing to Durban, I wanted to recruit a crew.'

Simon was humbled and embarrassed by the incident. His bills were enormous. It came at a time when Ethnée was preoccupied with her own plans—she was preparing to leave Africa permanently and emigrate to Australia. Her trip to Durban to help in the search for Simon had hastened her plans to leave three months ahead of schedule. She had already been planning to set sail from Durban in any case. She had been worried she would be sailing after a memorial for an adventurous and reckless son lost at sea. Instead, as she described it, she had the opportunity to spend some precious time with her son before she left.

So within a month of being reunited with Simon, Ethnée herself was setting sail—on an ocean liner bound for Perth. The journey on which Robert's strategic brain and financial skills had taken him was very different to where Simon found himself on the docks in Durban. While Ethnée has not disclosed what his financial circumstances were, Simon's friends reported that he had no idea how he was going to pay off the owners of the *Ville de Lyon*. And it was then, at his most vulnerable, that Simon's life would take an intriguing turn, one that Ethnée would become convinced contributed to her son's disappearance.

The Cold War Spy

1967–69

O conspiracy!
Sham'st thou to show thy dangerous brow at night
When evils are most free?
Julius Caesar, William Shakespeare

The European powers that had dominated Africa for about eighty years were retreating in the 1960s—colonial Britain's candle, for one, was sputtering to an end. But the era also marked the start of a covert campaign to counter the Communist-backed push for independence.

The colonial retreat lay the ground for the proxy wars—the West versus Communism—that would tear the region apart. British-backed spies worked hand in glove with the National Party, the hated government of South Africa. No matter what revisionist history may have been produced since, there's no escaping the fact that the UK, the US and Australia, along with the rest of the West, saw South Africa's National Party as a Cold War ally.

There was emerging civil strife and terrorism, be it state-sponsored or from those aligned with independence movements like the African National Congress (ANC) in South Africa. The ANC was agitating for the vote to overthrow the white minority. In Rhodesia President Ian Smith was about to illegally declare independence for his country in an attempt to entrench white minority rule.

It was chaotic. The region was flooded with intelligence agents. Simon was certainly known to the British embassy in Botswana and respected as a man of fearless mettle. He was of the right stuff too, with links to British peerage, no less.

It appears he first came to the attention of the spy network thanks to the man he'd worked with for all those years as a game warden: Patrick Bromfield. Bromfield was an old family friend but someone who Ethnée would later claim was wrapped up in the spy game too, as an agent for the British. It seems that even if Simon hadn't wanted to get involved, he didn't stand a chance.

Simon was hardly a political animal but his independence and resourcefulness made him an ideal candidate to be co-opted into Africa's underground network. Also, in stark contrast to his brother, Simon often found himself short of cash throughout his career. At the same time, he was not short of ambition. Did Simon ask his wealthy brother for help after his disastrous adventure on the *Carina*? Not according to his friends. Instead, Simon's desperate financial circumstances pushed him into the arms of the political machinery—the world of the South African secret service, the enforcers of apartheid.

Accounts differ as to the seriousness of the trouble Simon was in after returning to Durban. Apart from the heavy bills he would have to pay for being rescued, he was also facing the possibility of charges by maritime authorities after such a costly search and rescue mission—one that was precipitated more by Simon's misjudgement and inexperience than anything else.

Some said a wealthy family helped him out and refurbished his yacht in exchange for Simon taking them on a sailing trip up the east coast of Africa. But it was implausible—no one would trust a 28-year-old who had just sailed into awful trouble, and nearly died, to take them sailing.

Ethnée described how Simon's old Michaelhouse school-mates, in a touching sign of solidarity, were on the Durban docks to meet him when he was towed back into harbour, but there was someone else lurking in the background. A man they called 'Timber' Woodman. Woodman was an agent for the South African forces and, according to one of Simon's closest friends, he set about recruiting Simon.

Alan Hill, who once ran a taxidermy business in Maun, had come to know Simon well over the years—at one point during the 1970s Simon lived at his house in Maun. Hill, a hail-fellow-well-met kind of man educated at Cambridge, liked to describe Simon as a 'boys'-own Victorian hero'. 'He plunged in and did things. He had integrity and good morals,' he would say.

Some years after his disastrous episode on the *Carina*, Simon told Hill how he managed to pay his bills—he told Hill how Woodman approached him on the docks. The attention Simon's survival had received in the media alerted the authorities, including Simon's contacts in the British High Commission, to the fact that the time was ripe to recruit Simon for the Cold War effort. Hill would say: 'Woodman was on the Durban docks when they brought Simon in. Simon was in utter disgrace. He had committed all the evils a sailor could—sailing out without harbour permission and without being qualified.

'Woodman said to him: "Well, you're in deep kak [shit] here, old boy, aren't you? Tell you what, we'll do a deal. We'll refurbish your boat, kit it out, teach you to sail expertly and we'll be putting in the latest hi-tech equipment with a few little extra bits that you needn't worry about and we'll sail up the east coast."'

In other words, Simon was to captain a spy vessel up the east coast. It would stop in Tanzania's port of Dar es Salaam, a socialist country and sworn enemy of South Africa. South Africans call it the spook years, and finding a financially vulnerable chap—but an utterly fearless one—in Simon Holmes à Court was just the ticket for South African's spook department.

Simon did the deal. In all likelihood the man probably thought little of it or the political consequences of such a decision. That was his way: he had a problem and someone was presenting a solution. The *Carina* was refurbished, loaded with fishing gear and state-of-the-art listening equipment. Two men travelled with Simon in 1968 up the east coast as far as Kenya.

To this day their identity remains secret, although Ethnée remembered that a man by the name of Visser may have been involved. Ethnée would also maintain that Simon's east coast missions were before the disastrous Durban voyage. The evidence does not suggest this, since the weeks spent lost at sea occurred only eight months after he first bought the yacht and he had already spent some time in Beira learning how to sail.

Any mission up the coast would have taken some months, so it is almost certain to have occurred after October 1967, which corroborated Hill's version of events.

Simon's cover story was that they were just three men on a pleasure cruise. But it was a covert mission, a listening tour to spy on Russian ships in the area. These kinds of sailing missions were common in the sixties and seventies around the east coast of Africa, with South African agents acting like tourists on a long sailing holiday as a cover for anything from spying missions to bombing raids.

Ethnée would later say that Simon 'went up the east coast on a pleasure trip with two men but it was really a cover-up because they were doing all sorts of things like climbing aboard Russian ships in port'.

Hill was convinced Simon did not stay in the employ of the secret service long but little is known about this phase of Simon's life. But for at least two years it appears Simon was involved in reconnaissance work and, true to their word, the spies he was working with taught him to be a master sailor. He went from novice to expert, and became a master at celestial navigation. Whatever obligations he had to the spooks, it appears his contract was up in 1969 at which point Simon pursued something arguably even more ambitious. While his charter cruise business had come to naught, his east coast spy missions had given him a taste for long distance sailing. Released from any immediate obligations to the secret service, Simon sold the *Carina*, packed a small bag with his compass and sextant, and flew to London. He travelled down to England's sailing capital, Southampton, that same year and looked for a boat he was familiar with—another ketch like the *Carina*.

For a man who loved adventure, Simon, at the age of thirty, figured it was time to really test himself. He was going to sail around the world and make a film about it. He bought a 16 millimetre Bolex camera, a Nikon 35 millimetre still camera, and found a 30-foot ketch called *Maggie May II*. It had brilliant white sails and a white hull with a prominent blue stripe around the hull at deck level.

Simon wasn't the sort to say much but when he told the local Southamptonites he was going to sail the *Maggie May* around the world, they must have thought he was daft. A 30-foot bilge-keel ketch was hardly the stuff of long-haul ocean sailing—more like a day cruise on a Sunday afternoon for a retired gentleman keen on a glass of Pimms afterwards. He would prove everyone wrong. For the next three years he spent his life on the *Maggie May*, sailing around the world and eventually producing a remarkable film. But it would be no fairytale adventure and would offer clues to his subsequent disappearance. And while he was gone he would reflect on the Okavango Delta, a beating heart in the middle of Africa. He would miss the wildlife and would long to return. When he did it would be in vastly different circumstances.

A Caribbean Affair

1970–72

Ah love! Could you and I with Fate conspire
To grasp this sorry scheme of things entire,
Would not we shatter it to bits—and then
Re-mould it nearer to the Heart's desire!

The Rubáiyát of Omar Khayyam

When Simon set sail from Southampton in October 1969, he dreamed of commercial success for his film. But the thought of money somehow sullied his adventure too. He would later write:

> It took three years and 27,000 miles of sailing in a 30 foot yacht to make this film, then a further year of post-production work. The freedom and adventure has been sufficient reward in itself. The less savoury, but necessary reward has I hope yet to come.

Simon advertised in Southhampton newspapers for crew. Two young men replied. First was David Kitching, an English adventurer who had already travelled extensively through Africa, leaving England in 1959 when he was just 18. He was back in England and had the idea he'd hitch a ride to South America, or thereabouts, figuring he would try his hand at sailing. Save for some small dinghy sailing in north Cornwall he'd never before stepped on a proper yacht. The other response came from a Dutch man called Case (or *Keesje*). Neither of them knew of Simon's history as a sailor and his brush with death in southern Africa, which is probably just as well given what they were about to sail into. They left port in October 1969, bound initially for Barbados, via Lisbon and the Canary Islands.

Here we go again, thought Simon. A couple of days out of Southhampton and into the Bay of Biscay—they had warned me about these storms, and true enough, here she comes!

From the south-east the winds started to blow and what had been benign green-grey bumps were taking shape before him. Within hours, as the day was fading, dark monsters were rising to 40 feet, topped with white capped crests, angrily slapping the Maggie May.

This is a hell of a test early on, thought Simon, smiling grimly. Funny how Mother Nature always seems determined to mark the new chapters in my life. The old sea dog's hull was already shuddering at the impact of the waves and the winds were violent. He could see Case and Kitching were overwhelmed with the noise, as the guy wires screamed and the hull groaned. They were soon incapacitated with violent seasickness, spewing themselves inside out and finding a private hell on earth.

The Maggie May *was resolute and dogged, like her captain. The two of them were going to battle their way to Lisbon, no question.*

For two days it blew and Kitching and Case did what they could to help. But even when the wind finally abated it still left behind an enormous sea but at least it was now safe. Simon decided to hove to and let the Maggie May *drift. We'll have to get some sleep, he told them.*

He didn't show it but he was exhausted. He had been manning the tiller for nearly 48 hours. He collapsed in his bunk and strapped himself in.

'Don't worry about the swell, I think she'll handle it,' he said and promptly fell into a dead sleep. To the other two, the Maggie May *often felt like it was perpetually falling off a cliff, rising and falling on monster waves. Periodically the boat would be lifted and thrown down the face of cresting waves. Kitching told Case he felt like a dried pea in a tin. He was regretting ever setting foot on the yacht.*

Waking to a new dawn and calmer ocean, Simon and his amateur crew set about cleaning up the boat—the cockpit stank of vomit. 'You've had a baptism of fire,' Simon told them. 'But you'll never look back.' Later in Lisbon, Kitching and Case swapped stories with veteran sailors who had also just pulled into port. They too described the storm as one of the worst they had ever been through. The two young guns smiled at each other with pride.

They took on more supplies in Lisbon before sailing. Case had ran amok in port, as he would at subsequent landfalls. He was an extremely handsome young man, with long flaxen hair, a deep tan with bright blue eyes.

'Case and I would go off in the evenings and visit bars and generally look for fun, but Simon never accompanied us on these expeditions,' Kitching would later say. 'The women loved Case. He found little difficulty in finding companions.'

They sailed into the Canary Islands, at one stage becoming becalmed. One morning a large pod of whales were gambolling not far from the boat and Simon was soon off in a small inflatable dinghy, spending hours observing them at close quarters.

For days they remained becalmed. Bored, Kitching retrieved some chest expanders he had thrown into his bag. Leaning against his mast, Kitching started using the springs. Away on the horizon a large tanker was heading south but after a few minutes she changed course and was heading straight for the *Maggie May*. Kitching called Simon and Case to the deck and the ship sailed right past them.

'Are you alright?' a crewman on the bow shouted. 'We're fine,' they shouted back. Another man amidships asked the same.

Kitching would later say: 'Then as the bridge passed high above us an officer came out with a megaphone and shouted down to us: "If you do that again you will be charged £1000." It was only after they left that we worked out that my arm movements with the chest expander springs had been interpreted as the international distress signal.'

On the way to Barbados they passed through an enormous school of sardines—miles long, half a mile wide, the water boiling with the fish and their predators, including half a dozen or so Spanish trawlers, the fishermen cheering the *Maggie May* on into the south Atlantic. In 1969 a yacht sailing across the Pacific with a crew of young adventurers was still something of a novelty.

And then later, all three stood on deck for the remarkable sight of four huge water spouts to the north of them, all in a row as if marching west—in the same direction they were sailing.

Just before reaching Bridgetown, the men picked up the local radio station and had a good laugh at the current chart toppers. like: 'Bang Bang Lulu', 'Wet Dream' and 'Sell Your Pussy'.

Kitching would say: 'We came to the lee of Barbados at about three in the morning and were immediately struck by the wonderful smell of the island. Having been on the boat at sea for nearly a month the aromas were heady to say the least and we all sat on deck and watched as the sky lightened to a great day.' A Frenchman rowed over to them at daybreak and gave them fresh bread as a gift: the three of them wolfed it down.

Kitching farewelled Simon and Case in Barbados but not before one wild party around Christmas 1969. It was a beach party and about 30 people turned up drinking rum, which in those days cost about $US2 a gallon. A couple of hours into the party and Case had attracted the attention of a tall English woman and soon enough they were locked in a passionate embrace on the beach, disrobing and on the verge of sex just metres away from the party. Simon and Kitching pulled Case away when they saw the women's husband returning, a short fiery Welshman who had gone back to his boat for more drinks.

Someone told the Welshman what his wife was up to and without hearing the rest of the story, exclaimed: 'I bloody well know who that was,' and rowed out to a yacht. Some innocent chap who had been at the party emerged bleary eyed and was promptly punched in the face.

To Simon's reserved ways Case's behaviour was awful but he needed crew. They said farewell to Kitching and the two sailed on to Curaçao, a former Dutch colony that became the seat of government for the Netherlands Antilles in 1954. There they would recuperate and prepare the boat for its journey through the Panama Canal and on to the Galapagos and then through the Pacific.

Simon had intended to make the Galapagos, with its unique and unspoilt flora and fauna, the first act in his documentary, but he spent longer in Curaçao than planned. He was waiting on another crew member, Ron Wink, a sailing enthusiast Simon had met in South Africa around the time of his disaster on the *Carina* who, like Simon, wanted to sail around the world. While he was waiting for Wink, Simon crossed paths with another wayfarer on an adventure of her own.

In April 1970 Carin Timo, a Swede, was living on the shores of the Caribbean island when Simon sailed into Spanish Water, a beautiful and protected bay at the south-west end of the island. Attractive with fair cropped hair and a wide smile, Carin had fled Bogota, Colombia, with her two children. She had been living there with her husband but had recently divorced and feared the imminent elections—violence was predicted in Bogota during the poll. Carin and her two children sought sanctuary with a network of friends she had made in Curaçao after numerous holidays there.

She was excited when she found a cottage on the ocean front in Spanish Water. It would be a temporary stay as she was contemplating emigrating to Australia and would spend her time there sorting out the paperwork. It was on one of these long slow days, as the water lapped at her feet and her sons fossicked around the beach, that she spied a yacht in the distance. She watched as it sailed right into the bay and anchored just a few hundred metres away.

Simon and Case kept to themselves over the next few days. Carin woke each morning to hear them cleaning the boat and doing preparatory and maintenance work—it was obvious they were setting up for the next leg of a voyage. But it was soon apparent to Carin, curiously eyeing the intruders in her quiet cove, that the two men on board did not get along.

When their work had finished a few days later, Simon rowed across in his rubber dinghy with an enormous fresh lobster he had just caught. He looks like a real nature boy, she thought. He was wearing only khaki shorts and a deep tan.

Simon presented the lobster to Carin and asked her if she wanted it. 'Yes, I'll cook it for lunch,' she told him. 'But I want you to share it with me.'

The ice broken, Simon spent more and more time with her and her sons, Eric and John, then aged eleven and nine. They hit it off from the start, Simon glad to be off the boat and Carin welcoming this intriguing man. Simon explained to Carin that the *Maggie May* was such a small vessel, and the living conditions so cramped, that good humour could quickly evaporate. He said it was made all the worse when Case did not respect his property. Simon was fastidious and kept everything in perfect order. When Case once used Simon's coffee mug, it drew an extraordinary response: Simon refused to speak to him for a month.

Eric and John quickly formed a strong bond with Simon who, to them, was a real-life hero. With Carin, they sailed around the Caribbean Sea, exploring its coves and bays with scuba gear and snorkels. It was the start of a five-month adventure together. It would be nearly thirty years before Carin would appreciate the significance of their time together.

Simon was a strikingly fit man with hair bleached almost white by the sun and ocean, his skin a deep golden brown. There was not an ounce of fat on him. He was attuned to life at sea and lived on rice and seafood alone. With time on his hands before his Pacific adventure and filmmaking started in earnest, Simon and Carin looked all set for a holiday romance. Case in the meantime had disappeared—off partying on the island, waiting for Wink to arrive.

A whole new world opened up to Carin. Simon's knowledge of marine life was fascinating. He was adept at catching wildlife also. Once when they were diving together, Simon simply coaxed a trunk fish into his hand. At times like that Simon was in his element.

During these long, languid, sun-kissed days in the Caribbean, Simon spoke of his dreams. As their friendship grew Simon started to reveal more about his background and how his dream was to make a documentary and 'how he would make a fortune'. He also spoke to Carin about his brother Robert, telling her he lived in Perth and was 'very wealthy'. However, Carin found it difficult to get close to Simon—he was secretive and reserved, not the type to make friends easily. 'I think that was just the way he was. That was his personality,' Carin said.

But he did reveal to Carin more about another mysterious part of his life: that of being a spy. Simon told Carin how he was lost at sea on the *Carina* in 1967—and how some men approached him after he was towed into Durban. 'They wanted him to take them up the Mozambique coast and they would pay for his repairs,' she said later. 'They would sail along and pretend to be holidaymakers but they were the South African secret police, checking out developments in Mozambique.'

Simon was fairly low-key about it and Carin ended up teasing him, calling him 007. It appears he was off the secret service's payroll by then, however, and that his sailing venture around the world was not part of some ongoing mission with the spooks. On a couple of occasions Carin and Simon travelled to Curaçao so Simon could collect his regular pension from the British government—she would joke that it was part of his '007' contract but Simon assured her the pension he received was due to his retirement from the game department.

This enigmatic man intrigued Carin. In later years she reflected: 'He didn't seem to have any desire for worldly goods. He only ever dressed in khaki shorts. He probably only had one shirt which he put on if he had to go into town.' And he made her children laugh. On one occasion Simon flummoxed a local fisherman. The man had set a fish trap off a reef where

Carin's children had habituated a trigger fish—they would feed the fish regularly and it had become a pet. Spying the trap, and upset that their beloved fish might be caught and used as bait, they rushed over to Simon pleading with him to save their fish. He went with them to the reef's edge, hauled up the trap, cut a big hole in the net and threw it away into deep water.

They went home and Simon drank tea while he waited for the arrival of the fisherman who had put the trap there. Simon thought it funny to watch the confused fisherman walking around trying to find his trap. Simon and the children whooped with delight over the fact that they had saved the fish.

For some of their time together Carin was on crutches after wrenching her knee, and Simon spent a long time patiently teaching her to play chess—the game he and Muche had spent hours and hours playing in Francistown in the sixties.

With the azure waters lapping against the Caribbean shore, a love affair appeared destined for Simon and Carin, sun-bleached and carefree. Carin was not employed and they sailed during the day, and they would stop to dive for fish and crustaceans. Lazy days would drag into evening meals with a bottle of wine and, one would presume, warm loving. But it was a puzzling friendship, like many of the relationships Simon developed with people over his life. The mysterious Simon: he had an ability to make an impact on someone's life and then just slip away.

No, his time with Carin was not the perfect fairytale romance. There was to be no enduring love story. Over the months they were together Carin found Simon a difficult man to understand. He was secretive about his life and appeared afraid of committing himself. 'He was not open. No. Never,

never open.' Carin would say to him that he appeared to communicate better with animals than humans. She sensed Simon was already missing Africa and wanted to return. But Simon has always stayed in her mind—not least because he introduced Carin to sailing, which she has been doing ever since.

Finally Wink arrived and Case joined the crew again. It was around September 1970 and both Simon and Carin committed to stay in touch. He had given her a rough timetable and an address in Perth for mail. He told her he would be returning to Perth to complete the post-production work on his film. Over the next year Simon wrote regularly to Carin about his adventure and she wondered when she might see him again. In the meantime, she set about getting her life in order and the permanent home she chose was Queensland. They would meet again, but under very different circumstances.

With Wink and Case, Simon set sail for the Galapagos, through the Panama Canal. Simon wrote:

Leaving Panama, the *Maggie May* was swept along in the arms of a brisk north-easterly . . . taking us nearly 900 miles to the south-west before the islands, made legendary by the naturalist Charles Darwin, hove into view: the fabulous Galapagos. As our tiny yacht felt her way into the anchorage the stark volcanic cliffs loomed over us. There was an awareness of being watched and the alarm went out: the eyes that had witnessed wandering seafarers wading ashore for over nearly two centuries eyed our approach.

At the time the Galapagos were still a rare destination for filmmakers and Simon felt the early explorer's joy of discovery. He was conscious of man's insensitivity and the mistakes of the past. For example, he lamented how the Galapagos turtle had become such an easy target for sailors in years gone by.

> This turtle is a relic from pre-history and gave the island group its name. It's rare and protected by the government of Ecuador. They are 300 pound giants and were once slaughtered by the hundreds to provision ships; whole colonies disappeared. Now they watch us, inscrutable and unperturbed.

They spent their days filming at the Galapagos, capturing hours of footage before setting sail on a 5500-kilometre journey south-west to Polynesia, Simon evoking the Ancient Mariner in his account of the voyage:

> Following the lead of an albatross and spurred on by the trade winds we headed westward, leaving behind the unique and tiny sanctuary that triggered Darwin's radical theory of evolution and what followed until Polynesia was an endless procession of warm, sunny days and clear starlit nights.

Simon's itinerary was to spend a month or two in each island group, then about three to four weeks sailing to the next group. He had roughly planned the route and the islands had to be places he regarded as out of the ordinary to qualify for footage in his documentary—islands off the tourist map. It was the reason Simon decided against travelling to Easter and Pitcairn islands.

Simon was constantly looking for photogenic scenes but strangely, to Wink's mind, he never read a single book about photography, cinematography, scripts or screenplay. Wink could see Simon was a driven person, wanting to get places, achieve the photographic and sound recordings and then move on. Wink could not understand why he found it so difficult to just relax and enjoy the beauty and tranquillity.

Armed with his 16 millimetre Bolex camera, Simon shot footage the Western world had rarely seen. It epitomised the sort of pursuit Simon appeared to long for. While Robert was cutting another deal in the early seventies on his way to becoming Australia's first billionaire, Simon was sailing into some safe harbour on a remote beach in the South Seas, and climbing up a volcano to get a shot of a caldera. While Robert was buying Rolls Royces and the 400-acre farm that would be developed into one of the country's best racehorse studs, Simon was intent on filming the Pentecost vine jumpers in Vanuatu in 1971.

Wink could see how determined Simon was to capture everything he could and the lengths he would go to get a good shot. It was no holiday. Quite early on Wink appreciated that there were likely to be few light-hearted moments on board. Simon was utterly focused on the film. Wink would spend nearly two years on board the *Maggie May* with

Simon but, despite living in such close quarters, he never got to know the man. Like his brother Robert, Simon played his cards close to his chest. Later Wink made the startling observation that: 'In all the years I spent sailing with him, I do not recall him ever confiding anything about his personal life, nor was there a single conversation about his philosophies on life.'

Driven to succeed, his extraordinary journey was a mixture of passion and blind ambition. He ran a tight ship, paying meticulous attention to some things but also overlooking other things some would consider obvious—it frustrated his crew and sometimes it landed them in serious trouble. Close shaves were common. On one occasion the *Maggie May* was nearly run down by a freighter in the Pacific, a brush with disaster redolent of Simon's time on the *Carina*.

The *Maggie May* was slow and cramped but it did not seem to faze Simon like it did the other crew members. For Simon to sail this tiny vessel around the world took a tremendous amount of self-reliance, hardiness and courage that Simon's friends admired. Very few people could have done it.

Like Carin, Wink and subsequent crew members would say how Simon was extremely ambitious about his film project; nothing was going to stand in his way. He wanted a critical success and spoke of international acclaim once it was completed. Perhaps that is not surprising. Simon was not a material man but maybe he wanted to prove himself against the extraordinary career of his brother.

When the crew sailed into the waters of Pentecost Island, they would be among the first Western filmmakers to capture the extraordinary ritual that some maintain helped spawn one of the world's most popular adventurous pastimes: bungee jumping. The first film of the vine jumpers is a credit owed, indirectly, to the Queen of England, since she paid a honeymoon visit to the islands in the 1950s.

The islanders treated her and the Duke to a display even though it was autumn rather than spring, the usual jumping season. A newsreel film crew caught the action. Unfortunately, because the vines were more mature and less pliant, they broke in the course of one of the jumps and an islander later died as a result of the injuries he sustained. It was captured on camera by a newsreel team and was widely broadcast at the time.

Simon's footage of the Pentecost jumpers helped bring to popular culture what has become a rite of passage on the world's backpacking travel circuit, particularly in Africa where, for instance, a bungee jump off the rail bridge that crosses near Victoria Falls is now worn as a badge of honour.

Simon's own interpretation of the Pentecost vine jumpers befits any travelogue. He wrote of the ritual in the New Hebrides with sensitivity and a sharp eye:

> The New Hebrides themselves are a fascinating group of islands. They have the distinction of being a condominium, meaning that they are jointly governed by two nations, Britain and France.
>
> This gives them two governors, two administrations, two separate police forces (differently uniformed) and separate schools and so on.

One of the less developed islands in the group is Pentecost. The only sign of western encroachment here is the scattered missions and handful of plantation owners. It is here that one of the strangest pagan customs of the Pacific is still practised—the vine jumpers of Pentecost.

Each man cuts and secures his own vines. The jumps are done from different levels. The highest was 70 foot, and the lowest, done by a ten-year-old boy, was about 50 feet. An expert jumper will allow his head to just brush the ground before the vines jerk taut. A new tower is built each year and the ceremony takes place only when the vines in the bush reach certain elasticity. Small children, only a few years old, often practise jumps from their fathers' shoulders while being firmly held around the ankles. The final jumper from 70 foot was a great pessimist and he gave a long speech in pidgin English before jumping. He did not know how anyone could survive such a jump but obviously the thought of those big delicious yams spurred him on. As can be seen from the film he had a rough landing but he lived to enjoy his yams.

Simon spent a year in the Pacific, charting the anthropological customs that intrigued him most. He reported with an earnest attention to detail. At the Santa Cruz group of islands further north, Simon was intrigued by the use of a currency consisting of feathers, writing of the custom:

One of the rarest forms of currency still used in the world today is found on one small island in the Santa Cruz group.

Only on Ndeni Island is feather money made, and only a few select men know how to make it.

These men are chosen by their villages and spend their entire lives making feather money. They are exempt from all common village duties. Their houses are built for them and food regularly supplied.

Today feather belts are used mainly for bridal payments. A good wife will cost as much as five belts and the feathers from approximately one thousand sunbirds will go into the making of each of these belts. Only the brilliant red male sunbirds are caught and indignantly stripped of their beautiful plumage before being released to grow new feathers. The origin of the feather belt is not known, but the natives do maintain that at one time the feathers were merely stuck on ornate sticks and that these sticks were then used as currency, much as the belts are used today.

The early explorers make no mention of the feather belts but they do note that the natives had a great fondness for beautiful red flowers that are found on the island. Perhaps this fondness of colour led to utilizing of the brilliant red plumage of the unfortunate sunbird.

By the time they reached Bali in July 1972, Wink was ready to sign off, as was Case. But things were already in place for a new crew, thanks to Ethnée. She played a major role in assisting Simon through his journey, helping recruit the fresh blood for the Indian Ocean leg. Ethnée had settled in Perth in late

1967, after Simon's brush with death on the *Carina*, helping at Robert's new law practice.

She had visited Simon during his adventure, sailing with him around the Pacific for four weeks in a holiday-rendezvous in Fiji. She swam and snorkelled and lived off the sea for a month with her son and his crew, later saying that this time with her son and Wink was one of her most treasured memories. When she returned to Perth she placed advertisements in Australian newspapers to see what interest there was in sailing across the Indian Ocean from Bali—a less appealing journey compared with the island hopping that sailors can do through the Pacific.

And that's how a fast-talking, gun-running American came into Simon's life.

Diego Garcia

1972

Confidence. Every man wants to be determined.
Every man wants to believe in himself,
every man wants to be fearless.

Muhammed Ali

Gregg Lott had dodged the Vietnam draft in the late sixties and was spending his days, by his own admission, chasing women around south-east Asia and having the time of his life. In his early twenties he had given up his promising career as a budding restaurateur in the US and would never return there. Lott, from upstate New York, was an engaging man with huge charisma and he got through to Simon like few people did. He was just the kind of breath of fresh air Simon needed after nearly two years at sea.

Lott was working on laying a railroad in South Australia when he spotted the advertisement placed by Ethnée. He had arrived in Australia after an extraordinary year when he was forced to pay his way out of prison in Singapore for alleged gun-running. Lott had a disdain for authority and a fearless drive for adventure, and perhaps that put him on the same wavelength as Simon. After dodging the draft, Lott spent most of his time grafting in Taiwan and Hong Kong, and learning how to sail. Like Simon, he had had a few close shaves with death: in 1970 he was 'buried' by his family when he went missing, presumed dead, in the South China Sea after sailing through two typhoons. He finally drifted into the Manila yacht club in his stricken vessel, bedraggled and bemused at the attention.

It was around 1971 when Lott decided to sail further south and, with the blind optimism of the adventurous in their mid-twenties, sailed into a notorious pirate zone off the Philippines. These were the days before global positioning systems (GPS). 'It wasn't like we knew how to celestial navigate,' Lott would later say. 'We ended up tacking right into pirate territory. These pirates chased us for six hours and shot at us with machine guns.' Earlier, in Hong Kong, Lott had acquired a bunch of hi-tech devices then taking the world by storm—pocket calculators—and as he started getting more anxious about the territory he was entering, he started trading the devices for guns. It was a wise move.

'Luckily we had these guns because it saved our lives. They shot six rounds across our stern and came right upon us and we had this Mexican stand-off. This guy came up forward and raised his arm like: blast them out of the water. But they suddenly peeled away and took off because they saw we were armed and knew we were going to fight to the death.'

Lott then sailed to Singapore with a cache of weapons he had collected on board—the ignorance of youth; Singapore was hardly the place for a wayfaring Westerner with a cache of illegal weapons. Or, as Lott told his friends, 'Hey, we didn't know Singapore, no bell-bottoms, no spitting, no chewing gum and Lee Kuan Yew and the whole clean up the place thing.' Lott checked in to a hotel and, needing cash, starting selling some gear, like diving equipment. But he had his guns in his hotel room as well. A bellhop spotted them and informed management. Lott returned from a party at around 5 am and just after he'd shut his hotel room door it was bashed down and a bleary Lott was surrounded by military and police.

In a blaze of publicity, Lott was charged with gun-running and sentenced to a minimum of three years in the notorious Changi prison. He was in maximum security but, even in so-called incorruptible Singapore, he managed to get out after a few months. Lott paid $US6000 and was released. He was forced to catch the first flight out of Singapore and it was headed to Australia. Lott arrived at Sydney's Kingsford Smith airport, stayed quiet about his conviction and, to his surprise, was waved through. Before long he was necking beers in a pub in King's Cross, Sydney's infamous red light district.

Lott decided to stay in Australia and pick up some work, which is why he found himself working with a rail gang, pegging railway sleepers in outback South Australia. He spied the ad for crew on the *Maggie May* and a telephone number listed in Perth. He gave it a call and Ethnée answered.

Ethnée was interviewing the potential candidates, and already she had one other candidate—Perth resident Milton Skinner, then a 49-year-old and between jobs. It was a well-worn joke in the Skinner household, how 'Dad' was going to sail off on a big adventure for a few months and recapture some of the past he had spent with the Australian navy as a seaman during World War II. Skinner and his family goaded him after he read the advertisement that this could be the thing he was waiting for. Skinner spoke to Ethnée and she agreed he would make an ideal crew member. Skinner then helped Ethnée canvas potential crewmen and he was instrumental in selecting Lott.

Skinner, a stickler for detail, left little to chance. He did his checks on Simon as a sailor and he met with Robert, in his offices in Adelaide Terrace in Perth, to reassure himself about Simon's credentials. There would be weeks at sea across the Indian Ocean before any landfall, and Skinner was satisfied when Robert testified to Simon's ability—after all, he had already sailed some 30 000 kilometres and made it unscathed so far, Robert told him. Skinner had his reasons to be sure—a ship he sailed on during the war had been sunk. Skinner survived by clambering onto an inflatable life raft. He convinced Robert Holmes à Court to supply a similar raft for the *Maggie May*.

Meanwhile Lott, travelling with little more than the clothes on his back, was surprised to meet Skinner at the airport lugging around an inflatable life raft. Skinner managed to get it in the plane to Indonesia, despite encountering some reluctance from the airline staff. A bemused Lott helped Skinner heave it onto the plane as hand luggage, sitting at the back of the plane. The two made unlikely companions. Lott was yet to turn thirty but boasted a colourful history rivalling Simon's own, and he was ready for another chapter, keen to taste adventure again after long days hammering sleeper pegs.

They arrived in Denpasar and Simon met the men at the airport, dressed in a khaki shirt, shorts and sandals—about as formal as he ever got. They stayed in Bali for the next ten days, sorting out their supplies before setting sail; first stop was to be Christmas Island.

Lott thought Simon was a man 'straight out of Oxford' with his refined accent and no-nonsense approach. 'I went along with that at first but it did not take long for me to work out what he was really like,' he would later say. 'He was just a fun-loving guy, he just had that appearance about him. I never had a cross word with him, but then I was careful and did the right thing because I respected him a lot. Everything had to be done just right on board.'

Skinner regarded Simon as a true adventurer, admiring his stamina to have sailed so far already. There are not too many people who want to do what he did, Skinner thought. 'I sail purely because of my love for the sea. But not Simon, his focus was on the film,' he would say.

After arriving at Christmas and then Cocos islands, the three sailed in deep ocean for about two weeks. Deck watch was broken into three hours on and six off. They would cook the odd flying fish that landed on the deck or simply eat rice and the tinned food they had bought in Denpasar. Every third day meant cooking duties and Simon was undoubtedly the best cook. But he was a conditioned individual and rarely ate more than one meal a day. It was an old habit from his game warden days when he would walk for days on end in the African bush. Simon would just eat rice if it meant saving money on the budget for his film.

The *Maggie May* had four bunk beds below, two forward

and two aft, with the cockpit in the middle. Lott slept aft, Skinner portside forward and Simon starboard forward. It was cramped. They would strap themselves to the bunks in bad weather. Skinner adjusted quickly but Lott found it tough going and was violently seasick in the first few weeks. He thought the *Maggie May* was an 'awful and uncomfortable' boat. It made Simon's determination to sail around the world in it all the more remarkable.

The long journey across the deep Indian Ocean from the Cocos Islands is one both Lott and Skinner would remember as the highlight of their lives. And both would recount a time when they had feared for their lives thanks to their incursion into one of the most sensitive military zones in the world.

The *Maggie May* had started running low on supplies and water as they approached Diego Garcia, an atoll in the middle of the Indian Ocean between Indonesia and Africa. It was early morning and they laid off until sunrise before picking their way through the channel to sail into the lagoon. A speedboat soon approached and several British men in civilian clothes armed with semiautomatic weapons ordered them to hove-to. They demanded to board the vessel and check their ID. Only in recent years has the sensitivity about Diego Garcia emerged. The crew had sailed into the area just after the British had completed an extraordinary mission—the forced removal of thousands of villagers, the local Ilois, who they dumped in Mauritius.

Diego Garcia is a British territory but it is also the site of a US navy base under a British–US defence pact that was established in the early 1970s. It has played a central role in the Iraq Wars as a base for long-range bombers. Lott and Skinner still talk about the extraordinary sight in the lagoon—a village that had been in existence for hundreds of years was now nothing but a ghost town, with huts still standing and chickens running wild. They realised the villagers had been removed, which in itself was an extraordinary piece of information not known to the public at the time.

The British were officially denying there was any indigenous population on Diego Garcia. Secret Foreign Office memos that only emerged in 2000 during a High Court case in London brought by the disenfranchised Ilois refer to 'complete sterilisation' of the island. The 'sterilisation' started in 1968 and the last of the islanders were simply bundled onto ships and forcibly removed shortly before the *Maggie May* arrived in 1972. (Since then the Ilois had a victory in the courts in Britain for their cause to be repatriated to the island, much to the chagrin of the Americans since the base is vital to its aviation refuelling strategy for reconnaissance into the Middle East, as well as a home for some of its navy.)

Skinner said the British men boarded the *Maggie May* but refused to identify themselves. It was only after a tense few hours and a thorough search of the ketch that it emerged they were British naval personnel under strict orders to bar civilian entry into the Diego Garcia lagoon. Skinner, Lott and, especially, Simon were exceptionally nervous about the implications of their incursion into the area. The *Maggie May* could have been impounded.

They needed supplies and Skinner waited for his captain to speak but Simon was mute in front of the navy personnel. He would later recall: 'We didn't have much food. I spoke up. Simon was very frightened to speak and I just jumped in after I listened for a while—he was skipper and you don't speak above the skipper—but I said, look, we need some bloody stuff. And they said what do you need and we gave them a list and they came up with everything we wanted. They also gave us some American rations and we put them down in a locker in the bilge and water got in and washed all the labels off. It was a joke on board, we used to call it the lucky dip after that.'

The British gave them back their passports and they were allowed to sail into the lagoon. Not surprisingly, Simon was barred from filming but they were eventually cleared to stay for twenty-four hours. They sailed around the lagoon to the village. Lott and Skinner caught a couple of chickens and prepared a much-needed feast after more than a month at sea—only to find the chickens were as tough as old boots. Feral chickens and donkeys exist to this day on Diego Garcia, a reminder of villagers who once lived there. However, nothing of this extraordinary tale would make it into Simon's film.

Simon was keen to leave as soon as possible. The next day they set sail and headed to the Seychelles. It was where Skinner bade farewell to the two men, flying out to Perth via Mauritius. Lott and Simon then set a course for Aldabra, the island that would feature as the last sequence in the film of his journey. Simon wrote in 1974 of the Indian Ocean leg of the adventure:

The sailing route through the Indian Ocean is greatly lacking in island groups. In the approximate centre the Chagos Archipelago is now a closed American naval and communications base. It is not until one reaches the Seychelles that the island-feeling, so common throughout the Pacific, is once again felt. For some years now these beautiful islands have been opened up to large scale tourism and will one day be a tourist haven. But we sought the unusual and our haven lay 700 miles to the south on the British Indian Ocean territory of Aldabra. This wildlife paradise is today owned by the Royal Society, in London, which maintains a small, but efficient, research station on the island. Visiting scientists use its facilities to study unique fauna and flora in the unspoilt environment.

There was much to interest us here for this isolated coral atoll, together with the Galapagos Islands 20 000 miles away, are the only natural habitats of the giant tortoise.

Lott's capacity to hold his breath underwater was even better than Simon's and he helped secure some underwater footage as the two men dived on nearby Assumption Reef. Simon told Lott: 'In all the hundreds of places I've dived in around the world, some of the finest diving is here, right on my doorstep.' The footage of Lott shows him feeding fish and stroking them as if they were pets.

Simon's thirst for adventure was matched by his optimism that the film would be successful, enabling him to make his mark as a natural history producer and director. From Aldabra they sailed as fast as they could to Durban, about 3000 kilometres south-west, to get the film stock processed before it

Simon on joining the Botswanan wildlife department, around 1960.

Simon was an accomplished spear fisherman.

Simon in the early days, with his pet python.
PHOTO COURTESY ETHNÉE HOLMES À COURT

In Spanish Water, Curaçao, 1970.
PHOTO COURTESY CARIN TIMO

The *Maggie May* anchored in Spanish Water, Curaçao, 1970.
PHOTO COURTESY CARIN TIMO

Simon annoys the locals in Curaçao.
PHOTO COURTESY CARIN TIMO

Carin Timo on the *Maggie May*, 1970.
PHOTO COURTESY CARIN TIMO

Tim Liversedge.
PHOTO COURTESY TIM AND JUNE LIVERSEDGE

went bad. Once there, Simon busied himself trying to get things sorted out, including the sale of the *Maggie May*, to raise funds so he could continue to finance the project. Simon had hundreds of hours of footage.

Lott ended up staying on with the new owners of the *Maggie May* and sailed with them to South America. In those final weeks before they parted company, he and Simon attended a few parties but there was never any big celebration after eight months at sea together. 'I sailed off with the new owners to continue my circumnavigation and never saw Simon again. But he sticks in my mind all the time,' Lott would say.

After Durban, Simon flew to Perth and stayed with Robert and his family, and Ethnée, using the city as a base to complete the post-production work on his film in 1973. He also travelled to Indonesia to secure footage of the Javanese rhino. He lived rough for about three months in the jungle, trying to capture one on film, during which time the family never heard a word from him.

During this post-production work, Skinner met Simon for lunch one day in Perth. Simon told Skinner the editing of the film was going well. They discussed the journey over a few beers, laughing about Lott's awful seasickness in those first few weeks. Skinner didn't realise then, of course, but it would be the last time he would see Simon alive.

Reunited

1973–76

My soul, like to a ship in a black storm,
Is driven, I know not whither

The White Devil, John Webster

Robert offered to assist Simon in marketing his film, saying he could help him 'make a million'. 'What use would I have with a million dollars?' Simon asked rhetorically. However, friends of Simon said there was little doubt Simon was driven commercially, but he obviously wanted to do it his way.

Unfortunately, during the post-production of the film things started to go wrong. Simon had a mountain of footage but commercial success required great slabs of his three-year odyssey to be left on the cutting room floor. Simon decided to contact an old friend, Carin Timo. In the intervening years she had moved to Australia, settling in Queensland. Simon wrote to her on 18 July 1973, and he sounded an ominous warning about how the film might be perceived. 'The film was always going to run for 71 minutes and it had been planned and edited to that length,' he wrote. 'Last week we heard from the agents that 50 minutes would be a more saleable length for the overseas TV markets and that is the market I'm aiming for. To cut a long story short we have now re-edited the film and got it down to the required time.'

For Simon, the post-production work was a millstone, demanding seven days a week and leaving him no spare time. He finally headed to Melbourne to dub some sound and again wrote to Carin asking her to find for him a beach shack to rent for ten days when he had a break in his schedule. 'For the last six months,' Simon wrote, 'I have worked nearly every day on the film and when it's finished I'm going to be working hard to sell it, so I'm going to have an idle holiday for 10 days.'

Carin found him a place to stay—it was on Bribie Island, off the coast of Queensland. Simon spent ten days there alone. He was exhausted, catching up on sleep and taking long walks on the beach. In truth, he feared his project was collapsing around him. Carin, then living in Brisbane, travelled up to see him.

'I felt, in a way, disappointed, because we were two old friends but he was more withdrawn than before and I felt he was not a happy man. Obviously the situation had changed. He talked very often about his brother and that his documentary was not going to bring him success and fame,' Carin would later say. He had told her several times that he wanted to make a film that would provide a bit of his own success. He wanted his own income. He had hoped the film would underwrite his success so he could return to Botswana and pursue wildlife photography. He told Carin how Australia was a 'cold place'. But Carin felt there was little in common between them anymore. Simon had always seemed withdrawn but now she thought he had become quite cynical. There were none of the carefree days they had shared on Curaçao. That magic had gone.

Carin did not stay with Simon, deciding to leave him to his thoughts. Days later she returned to take him to the airport. Their conversation was strained. 'No one said anything about staying in touch . . . I didn't say anything, he didn't say anything. I think we both understood.'

She never heard from Simon again.

Over the years, Carin had always assumed Simon was alive and well in Africa, presuming their friendship was just one of many Simon had left behind in his travels and that he had gone back to Africa, living out a life in the bush he loved.

Simon settled on a name for the film: 'Maggie May, A True Life Adventure Film'. He published a brochure to advertise it; and included a heartfelt acknowledgment to those he had filmed and his crew.

Thanks must be given to many people. The majority will never read this, because they cannot read. They will never see this film about themselves because they live on remote unspoilt islands. They are simple and happy people and we thank them for their genuineness and hospitality so freely given. The various crews on Maggie May played an important part in making this film. Special thanks go to Ron Wink, who patiently climbed volcanoes and waded through tropical jungle in the interests of cinematography; to Gregg Lott, who held his breath longer than was possible so that the underwater footage could be taken; and to Milton Skinner, who helped in sailing across the Indian Ocean.

It was Simon's crowning achievement. Simon had sailed around the world, more than 43 000 kilometres, in a yacht hardly built for a world tour. His quest to film life, interpret it and understand it was unique at the time, considering that popular Western culture for a man his age was more about flower power, pot, LSD and women's liberation. None of that interested Simon. His 'trip' was a four-year adventure on the high seas.

He wanted to create on film an anthropological *tour de force*, in much the same way wildlife documentaries today are cut, and for a man of no experience it was an exceptional effort. Although the film contains some extraordinary footage— including an island tribe's sacrifice of a pig by strangulation after which an islander stands knee deep in the ocean feeding the pig's entrails to sharks without any apparent fear of being attacked—the end result fell well short. It lacked any personal touch. Perhaps Simon's shy nature did not help. He rarely appeared in the film and the narration was wooden and in the third person, never mentioning his name or those of his crew and the extraordinary personal journey they were all under-taking. Instead the film focused on anthropological and natural history anecdotes from around the Pacific Islands, but all at an arm's length.

A musical score is dominated by a flute player, a popular choice for documentaries in the seventies, only interrupted occasionally by the narration, which would have been so much better if Simon himself had explained his drive to sail so far to discover the treasures of the Pacific. But Simon was not a self-indulgent man and any attempt to personalise the adventure would have been anathema to him—one can see he had lofty ambitions for the film in his sensitive portrayal of the places he visited and the indigenous peoples he met.

The man's abiding love for nature can be heard at the end of the film. As the film closes on the island of Aldabra, the coral atoll in the Indian Ocean that to this day remains untouched by man, the narration gives tribute: 'Cruising in the *Maggie May* we have seen many cultures and customs far different from our own. We sincerely thank those people of all colours and creeds who gave us their hospitality, who allowed us to watch and sometimes share in beliefs and rituals so strange to our own way of life. We have learnt to respect these people as we have learnt to respect nature. Now the *Maggie May* tugs restlessly at her anchor, it's time to move on.'

If nothing else the film offers one remarkable glimpse of Simon's utterly fearless interaction with nature. On the Indonesian island of Komodo, where the twelve-foot komodo dragons have been the stuff of legend for passing sailors for centuries, Simon is seen approaching one which is in the process of tearing apart a wild boar. He has a stills camera in one hand and, armed only with a stick, he crawls close enough to the animal to reach out and pat the monster on the head.

The animal hardly flinches as it continues to feast on its catch. Komodo dragons have the ability to tear a man's arm off and yet Simon was confident enough to take a few photographs, as well as the movie footage featured in the film. Few people would ever attempt something as dramatic as this, and yet Simon's film makes little of what some would call bravery, others recklessness.

The problem for Simon was that he had never been a filmmaker. Wiser heads might have learnt more about the craft before attempting such an ambitious task. He secured no big distribution deals to international markets or to domestic television stations. 'The problem was it never got the exposure it deserved,' lamented Lott. 'Simon edited it himself, and chose the music himself—he did the whole thing by himself. For his situation that's all he could do because he didn't have the money. But I remain proud of Simon for pulling it off.'

Rather than give up on his film altogether, Simon headed back to South Africa and started selling the film himself— the hard way. He was determined to take it to the public. He became a one-man distribution outfit. He bought a VW Kombi van and travelled alone around the country showing his film in community halls. Carin would later say Simon's do-it-yourself travelling film show was not the picture he had painted of the film's market when he was in the Caribbean in 1970 at the start of his odyssey. Clearly, Simon's high hopes had been dashed. But it was hardly a mainstream documentary and so did not attract a mainstream buck. Perhaps, given the extraordinary appetite for adventure films and wildlife documentaries now, Simon Holmes à Court was ahead of his time.

Around late 1974 Simon travelled back to Botswana and screened his film at Muche's place in Francistown. It had been five years since anyone in Botswana had seen Simon. Liversedge travelled from Maun to catch up with his old friend, as did others. Simon then took his film to Maun too, screening it there on several occasions before realising it was time to pack it up and move on to something else. Rather than pursuing the filmmaking business after investing so much time in it, Simon decided to change tack. The problem was that Simon was broke. His brother, then establishing Bell Group as a public company and the vehicle that would earn his fame and fortune, sent him money but just how much is unclear. Simon still had his pension from the game department, then worth about £25 a month—which was enough to live on.

Simon turned to his old friend Bodo Muche for help. He decided he would try his hand at sculpting and Muche's technical expertise was unsurpassed in Botswana. Simon had always had a talent for clay modelling, winning a prize in primary school and applause from his teachers, who predicted he would become a famous sculptor. From around 1975 he started sculpting in earnest, and in 1976 spent time in Hartbeespoort Dam, north of Johannesburg, learning how to cast from an Afrikaner called Joubert. He rented a small room nearby in a cheap and grubby hotel.

Towards the end of 1976 he decided he would establish a foundry in Maun. He rented a shack near Croc Camp, on the outskirts of the town. It would be Simon's final place of residence and a fateful one.

Simon started to make some headway with his sculpting. He put the experience of the film behind him and in between getting lessons from Muche in Francistown, he spent time at a foundry in Johannesburg and modelling at the shack in Maun. Simon clearly had a natural aptitude for the art. 'He was determined and talented,' Liversedge would tell friends. 'He thought this is his way to make money and he was now going to become a great sculptor. That put him on a new trajectory.'

Now, perhaps, there was finally a sense of security around what he was doing as he worked away in his shack, moulding the materials. Maybe a life of wandering had given him a lifetime's physical experience to draw on: a muse, an inspiration. Was it an increasingly more tangible sense of satisfaction when he carved a true line, as he strived to trace an elephant's casual gait? Were his spirit and soul finally finding some comfort as he lost himself in his work? In this period Simon was doing some of his best work and maybe there was a heightened sense of confidence about his ability to deal with outsiders attempting to breach his realm.

His was a life built around the bush and the sea; a life of few possessions and a seamless interaction with nature. This gift he carried into his sculpting. Given the work he produced in this short period between 1975 and 1977, sculptors like Muche and Kent Ullberg, who also spent time in Maun, thought he could have become one of the greats in wildlife sculpting. Ullberg, a Swede, lived in Maun in the sixties and was attracted to Africa to learn the art of taxidermy and sculpting. He would become celebrated for his work in his adopted country of the US, and is now regarded as one of the best bronze sculptors in the world, producing bronzes of huge scope such as life-sized bison and his latest project, an eagle with a six-metre wingspan. Like others, Ullberg can't understand why Simon disappeared.

But many of his friends have wondered if it had its roots in late 1976, when things started to change dramatically for Simon. It was when he started become friendly with Daphne, his neighbour. She had moved from the north of the Delta separating from her husband, Bernie Truter, as their relationship soured, bringing her son Grant with her to find work in Maun. Daphne began flirting with a man open to her charms. Suddenly, just a few months before he disappeared, Simon had become as animated as anyone had ever seen him.

The Big Five

Christmas 1976

I met a lady in the meads
Full beautiful—a faery's child
Her hair was long, her foot was light
And her eyes were wild
La Belle Dame sans Merci. A Ballad, John Keats

Liversedge and his wife June asked Simon, along with a bunch of other friends, to celebrate Christmas and New Year on their riverboat, *The Sitatunga*, a 25-tonne beast that Liversedge built in the early 1970s. It served as a mobile viewing platform for research, photography and tourists. On the Okavango River near the town Shakawe, north from Maun, they gathered and partied. It was then that Simon, who to this point had had few intimate relationships, started a passionate affair with Daphne.

Daphne was one of six daughters of the famous African hunter Bobby Wilmot. In 1976 Daphne, with a marriage on the rocks, had been eyeing her handsome neighbour and now on the boat felt she was in the presence of a 'real Camel man', as she used to describe him, a reference to those cigarette advertisements depicting a rugged, husky adventurer. Daphne, a stunning brunette with soft brown eyes and tanned skin, had a reputation for being a man-eater. As one of the Wilmot girls she was someone to be reckoned with—it was in her genes.

Her father Bobby was a god in Maun in the forties and fifties. He was revered by all the old-timers then and is still talked about around campfires to this day. He was tough and wiry, all sinew as tough as papyrus. His father Cronje had been one of the first settlers in the area. It made Bobby a second generation white Botswanan—one of the few. His knowledge of the land was unsurpassed and he was a ruthlessly efficient hunter. He, along with another hunter, John Seaman, halved the Delta between them in the late fifties to late sixties and in a ten-year cull nearly wiped out the Delta's crocodiles. Times were different then and conservation of crocodiles was not an issue—no one ever seriously thought the crocs would disappear. This two-man hunting industry helped feed an appetite around the world for croc skins. It was reckoned about 25 000 crocs were wiped out over the period. Their numbers have still not recovered.

Bobby met his end in a way that befitted his life in the bush. He was bitten by a black mamba snake and was buried outside Maun on the banks of the Thamakalane River. It was deemed hallowed ground for both whites and blacks in Maun, who respected him as an elder of the Delta.

Bobby Wilmot left one other legacy. This rough diamond raised the Wilmot girls, who grew up as tough as their dad but had one other star quality: Daphne and her sisters were beautiful. They were vivacious and charming and the Delta's hunters—who might stare down a charging lion, elephant or buffalo with a steady aim and a calculating mind—would go weak at the knees when it came to the Wilmot girls. In a small town like Maun, where men outnumbered women fifty to one, the competition for women was intense.

These men, used to trophy hunting in the Delta, took the same approach when trying to add the Wilmot girls to their rollcall of conquests. The 'big five' in hunting parlance refers to lions, buffalo, leopards, elephants and rhinos. When it came to the Wilmot girls it meant something else. Four of Bobby's daughters—Daphne, Joyce, Eileen and Hazel—were chased by the men, and a Wilmot cousin, Ursula, was much sought after too: the Big Five. They were third generation white women in Botswana who knew how to shoot a crocodile just as well as the next 'man'. 'Sexy bush girls' is the way the men used to describe them. All the men tried it on but the Wilmot girls knew how to handle them—they were just as tough and uncompromising.

Having such a well-known father who was a friend to so many in the Delta meant they lived in the Delta like they owned the place. And they were before their time, doing all the things the men could do, only looking like pin-up girls while they did it. There was nothing quite like watching one of the Big Five in action.

Daphne, twenty-nine, was a feisty woman and the most popular. Simon might have been one of the most fearless men in the Delta but, like the others, when Daphne turned her sights on him, he was helpless.

It was to be a fun-filled and boozy Christmas and Simon, possibly in the first real blush of love at thirty-six, was utterly reckless. He was doing things sober that his friends would only consider when blind drunk. During their week on the river, Simon thought nothing of diving from the bow of the houseboat and plunging into the cool Okavango River, despite being eyeballed by crocodiles on the opposite bank—six metres each of honed, amphibious killing machine.

They all knew Simon was fearless, but to jump in the river when there were crocs around was crazy. As the houseboat chugged forward Simon would drift past the hull on a five-knot current, with Daphne and friends peering over the side. He would grab a trailing rope and pull himself up at the back of the boat.

Daphne eyed her new flame, who was wearing only well-worn khaki cotton shorts. With his golden brown hair, blue eyes and broad shoulders of a seasoned swimmer, years of safaris and living rough in Africa had cut him a solid physique.

Simon, devil-may care, strolled up to the bow again and, before Daphne could stop him, dived off. 'Simon!' she shouted. Simon surfaced, smiling, and drifted down once more before Daphne implored: 'Simon, really, it's stupid, the crocs are everywhere.'

There was one occasion—a fixed look on his face, jaw clenched—when Simon began quickly swimming for the rope. He caught it with his right hand and hauled himself fist-over-fist and, in just a few seconds, grabbed the bar on the stern and lifted himself out of the water and over the side. As he did, just yards away, a huge croc bobbed to the surface. Simon looked shaken at first, and then shrugged the incident off with a smile.

That Christmas was the start of a passionate and rocky four-month affair. After the houseboat trip they went back to Croc Camp and most evenings they would watch the sun set while floating on a tractor tube down the Thamakalane, drifting in and out of the reeds, and with their goggles explore the crystal clear waters. But there was one small problem. Daphne was still married to one of the gentlemen of the Delta, Bernie Truter. Everyone liked Bernie but it wasn't long before whispers of the Christmas affair filtered back to him. It was a kick in the guts for him.

Daphne and Simon had known each other vaguely over the years without any attraction in the past. But Daphne was impressed by how worldly Simon had become, and the funny stories he had to tell. She used to tease him about a big brown stain on the pair of shorts he habitually wore. Simon would tell her: 'Well, I'm lucky enough to have a brown stain from a Javanese rhino on my shorts, so I don't want it out!' Simon spoke of the beauty of Bali and gave Daphne an enchanting talisman made of pearl, with a small face carved in it.

But Daphne and Simon, even in their brief time together, had some vicious arguments. Daphne was a freewheeling woman in Maun in the 1970s, and Simon was about to get badly burnt. He was caught completely out of his depth. He might have been able to handle the seas and the bush, but not feisty women like Daphne. That was certainly a challenge for a man who was very shy. On a trip they took together to Johannesburg, a trivial matter exploded into a slanging match and each refused to give ground. Simon finally broke the silence when they passed a huge expanse with a lone tree in the distance. 'See that tree out there, Daphne? That's me.'

After Simon's disappearance, it didn't take long for some of the Maun locals to start whispering that perhaps Bernie had had something to do with it.

Liversedge met with Bernie and they spoke at length about Simon. There had been the tall tales over beers at Riley's Pub that maybe Bernie had kidnapped him. For one, Bernie explained, it was unlikely he could have overpowered a man like Simon and, anyway, Simon's car was found in South Africa. Did anyone seriously believe he could have driven down to South Africa's southern coast and back without being noticed? That was a week-long journey. Truter hadn't left Shakawe. It checked out. Liversedge and townfolk soon dismissed the possibility of Bernie's involvement.

Liversedge met with Daphne, trying to glean from her a lead on why Simon might have left Maun—apart from his stated aim to other friends that he planned to pick up sculpting supplies in Johannesburg. There must have been some explanation for him to drive so far south. Liversedge spent hours grilling Daphne, feeling that maybe there was something she was not letting on.

Finally Daphne did offer one theory—it was a long shot. She revealed she and Simon had not been on the best of terms when he left. They had had a lover's tiff the night before. She told Liversedge he'd gone off in a huff. Simon's connection to the sailing community could be a clue, she said. Maybe he had abandoned his car on the coast and had hitched a ride on a yacht to sail to Perth to see his family. He was capable of that kind of thing. 'What about his car?' Liversedge said. Possessions meant nothing to him, and it was a cheap old Datsun anyway, Daphne replied. 'Simon probably wanted to turn the tables on me,' she said.

'There was a row over where the relationship was headed. Simon wanted a commitment but I was getting cold feet. When we woke that morning he said little. He made a cup of tea, just watching me go about my morning chores and getting Grant ready for school.

'Then, Simon quite deliberately put his cup of tea down on the table and walked out muttering something about heading to Johannesburg. I was thinking, maybe we'd see how we felt about each other when he got back. And I let him go, I didn't follow him out. If anything I was relieved that I had some space to think things through. I was wondering how I could end the relationship. Simon was putting pressure on me.'

And Bernie was due to come back to Maun from his base in Shakawe. Everything was still so raw. Daphne said she had rushed into things with Simon. 'I didn't want to be tied up. Obviously the relationship had deteriorated with Simon to the extent that I didn't really want to be with him all the time.'

She was a tough woman, Daphne, Liversedge thought, and she would have put her view in no uncertain terms. And Simon sailing off to Perth sounded a plausible explanation. He knew how sensitive Simon was when it came to affairs of the heart. He had not been with many women. He recalled a time when, in his early twenties, Simon was smitten with a young woman in town but before he could muster the courage to ask her out she promptly announced her engagement to someone else. Simon went bush in despair, spending weeks by himself in the wilderness.

But Daphne was so worried about Simon's whereabouts she had sent a telegram to the Holmes à Courts. She kept it relatively cryptic in the mistaken hope it would not unduly worry Ethnée, who was well known to them all as a respected pioneer from her days establishing the Chobe lodge. Daphne wired the following telegram around June 1977, before Simon's car had been found: 'Simon, Big Tube and I are missing you. Where are you?' She signed it Frog, Simon's pet name for her. Big Tube was a reference to the tractor tyre they had used on the Thamakalane River.

But for Ethnée, now sixty-one and living on Robert's expansive horse ranch south of Perth, the obscure message was disconcerting. As someone who dabbled in spirituality, the telegram filled her with a sense of foreboding that something was gravely wrong. She thought about whom she could call in Botswana—she had no idea who 'Frog' was. It had been nearly ten years since she had last been there. Robert told her not too worry. Clearly, Simon had once more gone bush without telling anyone. He'd turn up again, he said.

Simon was amazed at just how cold Daphne had become. Once back at his shack, Simon put two jerry cans into the back of his Datsun, tossed in a windbreaker and his leather satchel containing his passport. He settled in behind the steering wheel and threw his

car into reverse. The fine Delta sand swirled in the Datsun's cabin, shafts of morning light catching the gritty mist. Simon's left hand rested atop the seat while his head was turned, chin resting on his shoulder to peer through the rear window. The differential on the Datsun pick-up whirred as he reversed, bouncing over the ruts of his sandy driveway.

He started to swing the car about but he stopped abruptly, watching the airborne path of dust wrap itself back around the car and then fade as it settled to the ground on this windless day. His gaze switched for a last look at his home.

Life in the rondavel, his circular one-bedroom reed house with its thatched roof, was a bit primitive, but having lived in cramped conditions on the Maggie May, it was relative luxury, really. His landlord was Daphne's brother Lloyd. Bloody Wilmots, Simon thought, and smiled wryly. The town's legends and death-defying feats were not the only things they laid claim to!

Scattered about was the flotsam and jetsam of his sculpting work. Some moulds sat on a makeshift shelf, alongside empty bags of plaster. Through the rondavel's timber-framed window the sun streamed, highlighting inside his plasticine model of his last work— an elephant standing half a metre tall. He had worked for months on the piece and it was finally ready for casting. It was a serene composition, capturing the spirit of Africa's most relaxed and honourable creatures.

Simon broke the reverie and with his open hand pushed the gearstick into first. He headed out onto a well-worn dusty track to Maun, about fifteen minutes away. He crossed through the mopane woodland and through leadwood and acacia trees.

His car rumbled over a tired bridge over the Thamakalane; he smiled at the thought of all the locals who had joined the 'Croc

103

Club' by missing the bridge when they were too drunk at the wheel to care. All of them managed to survive the plunge down the bank and the mad scramble back up to escape the jaws of a resident crocodile that, like a troll, lived under the bridge.

Simon hit the main bitumen road into Maun, the vista widening to open scrub as the road left the more temperate zone created by the flooding of the river: a yearly event that brought the locals, black and white, together to watch the first trickle of water course its way into Maun.

He looked into the rear-vision mirror, watching the riverbed, its vegetation, his shack, all speeding away from him.

Ethnée's Quest

1977

Ah, moon of my delight who know'st no wane,
The moon of Heav'n is rising once again;
How oft hereafter rising shall she look
Through this sane Garden after me—in vain

The Rubáiyát of Omar Khayyám

Liversedge, a man with strawberry-blond hair, a strong jaw and long sideburns befitting the era, was terrier-like in his determination to find his friend. He had time on his hands. The police in South Africa were moving slowly. He and June had just sold out of their partnership in *The Sitatunga*—it had not proved to be the money-spinner they had hoped for. Liversedge was on the lookout for another project. He dabbled in sculpting too and, like Simon, was an amateur filmmaker, but for the next few months locating Simon was his only thought.

Daphne had heard nothing since sending the telegram. When news of the car's discovery reached Maun it was decided by police and friends that Liversedge should be the one to make the fateful call to the Holmes à Courts in Perth. Late one night—it was now around early July 1977—Ethnée answered the phone and her worst fears about her son came true. 'We thought maybe he was with you,' Liversedge said to her. He then told her about the state Simon's car was found in. The news knotted Ethnée's stomach and suddenly she felt as if a cold wind was blowing through her soul.

Liversedge and Robert spoke and they both made much of Simon's wayfaring ways but there was no denying the strange circumstances regarding Simon's car, with its licence plates removed and engine numbers bashed off. It looked bad. 'We'll employ an army to find him,' Robert told Liversedge, who was in touch regularly over the next few weeks—gloomy late night phone calls to Robert's stud at Keysbrook with the same refrain: no news.

Ethnée called everyone she knew in South Africa and Botswana but no one had heard from Simon. It was now late July and critical time had been lost. Ethnée also spoke to the Port Elizabeth police regularly. If Simon had enemies, they told her, they had bought a lot of time by hiding Simon's car in the bush and concealing its identity. Ethnée held to the hope he would simply turn up on someone's doorstep—that's how he usually arrived, quietly appearing without fanfare and with little fuss.

The media, otherwise distracted by the incredible events brewing in the country, were finally alerted to Simon's strange disappearance in August as the police slowly pieced together the story of the car's owner and his family, and started to mobilise a public campaign for information. On 24 August

1977 the *Eastern Province Herald* in Port Elizabeth headlined a report: 'Police baffled over sculptor'. More reports followed during the next week, describing Simon as a powerfully built, stocky man, about 169 centimetres in height, with fair hair and complexion and blue eyes.

On 27 August, Major van der Merwe was quoted in the newspaper giving more details about the discovery of the car and how 'the vehicle seems to have stood there for some time before it was found; the back tray was already full of leaves. There is no record of it having been stolen either in this country or in Botswana.'

While the forces assured her everything was being done, Ethnée told Robert she felt powerless so far away and that she must travel back to South Africa. She would help search for her son. Robert agreed and would foot all the bills. Her arrival in South Africa might also trigger more interest in the media. She told Liversedge of her plans and they arranged an itinerary.

Ethnée packed her bags. Robert's work commitments prevented him from making the trip but he still suspected Simon would arrive on someone's doorstep soon enough. Ethnée prayed that maybe a mother's intuition might help in tracking Simon down. With Liversedge, Ethnée would travel around South Africa and Botswana looking for clues.

From Western Australia Ethnée travelled home to a country half the size of her adopted state but one with a world full of problems. Compared to the stable, peaceful west coast of Australia, where the majority live their days in suburban bungalows hugging the coast in the south-west corner, what was to confront Ethnée Holmes à Court in South Africa was a shock. She was flying into a country just as it was about to hit one of the biggest turning points in its history—let alone in the history of the twentieth century. A tragic sacrifice to political freedom was being made.

Steve Biko's life had started to ebb away on the floor of a Port Elizabeth jail on 11 September 1977 before he was dumped naked in the back of a Landrover and driven 1500 kilometres north to Pretoria. He died in a Pretoria hospital the next night, 12 September. The beating and the poison his captors subjected him to during his three-week ordeal became the seismic event in what was known as The Struggle. If there was a catalyst to the end of apartheid in South Africa, it was Biko's death. The country had already started to buckle politically the year before in the 1976 Soweto riots.

There was an explosion of grief and vibrant colour as 15 000 Africans of all ethnicities gathered at Biko's funeral and mourned the loss of a natural leader. The regime had created an identifiable martyr, an axis around which the struggle for democracy would always centre. Biko's death was the stuff of solidarity for the splintered and factional black groups. The political institutions apartheid created started to rock, and the edifices to crumble. In the rubble, new institutions have been erected and the people have Biko's memory as a touchstone.

Against these turbulent events the story of Simon Holmes à Court's disappearance seemed destined to be lost. Biko's death was dominating the news but Ethnée's trip helped lift the profile of her son's disappearance. She arrived in Johannesburg on 13 September, making the long journey across the Indian Ocean from Perth.

Liversedge, wearing a gull-collared white shirt with a

Simon was an excellent sculptor.
PHOTO COURTESY JOE MYBURGH

Liversedge at work.
PHOTO COURTESY TIM AND JUNE LIVERSEDGE

MISSING YACHT SEEN

DURBAN.

THE missing yacht, Carina, which left Lourenco Marques on October 13, has been seen along the coast near Scottburgh, sailing towards Durban. Only the skipper, Mr Simon Holmes Acourt is on board.

The Durban harbour radio station alerted all vessels along the coast to be on the look-out for the 31-foot ketch, which has a white hull and blue mainsail. So far no reports have been received from ships that the Carina has been spotted.

The harbour captain, Captain McKinnon, said last night that it might well be that the yacht was carried off course by a strong wind. 25 OCT 1967

MOTHER ANXIOUS

A Salisbury mother was shocked last night to be told that her 27-year-old son was more than ten days overdue in a single-handed yacht voyage from Lourenco Marques. Mrs Ethnee Holmes Acourt said a relative

PLANE AIDS IN SEARCH FOR KETCH

26 OCT 1967

Herald Correspondent
DURBAN.

SHIPPING and aircraft, including a S.A.A.F. Dakota from Youngsfield, Cape, had by last night reported no sign of the missing ketch Carina, due in Durban last week from Lourenco Marques.

The 31-foot ketch, sailed by Mr Simon Holmes-a-Court, a Botswana game ranger, was reported sighted for about two hours off Scottburgh, 40 miles south of Durban, on Tuesday afternoon, but she has not been seen since.

Mr Jimmy Whittle, a Durban boatbuilder, who had been asked by a friend in Lourenco Marques to look after Mr Holmes-a-Court when he arrived in Durban, became alarmed on Monday at his failure to arrive and notified

Yachtsman found off Bashee

Herald Correspondent
28 OCT 1967
DURBAN.

SIMON HOLMES A'COURT, the 28-year-old lone yachtsman who has been missing in his ketch, Carina, for the past three days, is safe aboard the French vessel, Ville de Lyone and is being brought to Durban.

The yacht, dismasted by the wind, is being towed by the 9,715-ton French vessel which sighted her at about 3 p.m. just north of the Bashee River mouth. Mr Holmes A'Court a former Michaelhouse boy and now a Botswana game ranger, was said to be "fine".

The finding of the Carina brought to a close a three days air and sea search in which a S.A.A.F. Dakota took part and all shipping operating along the coast kept a close watch.

The Ville de Lyone, on a voyage from Dakar to the Persian Gulf, radioed to the port office in Durban that she had sighted the yacht.

Later a second call came

A mother's joy — missing son is safe

28 OCT 1967

A hasty flight from Salisbury to Durban ended in joy for Mrs ETHNE HOLMES A'COURT last night when she was told her son Simon, who had been missing in his ketch, Carina, was safe and on his way to Durban.

Mrs Holmes A'Court was told of her son's disappearance on Tuesday night after a friend had heard a radio news report.

Her plans to travel down to Durban before going overseas for an indefinite period in December were speeded up by three months. Mrs Holmes A'Court had to sell her furniture and car, pack her belongings and arrange an air passage to Durban in a matter of two days.

When told that her son was safe, she said: "I am delighted." She had always feared for her son, as Simon had been a game ranger for several years—a dangerous job.

Mr Holmes A'Court, 28, is safe aboard the French vessel, Ville de Lyon, and is being brought to Durban.

The yacht, dismasted by high winds, is being towed by the 9,715-ton French vessel which sighted her at about 3 p.m. yesterday just north of the

Simon's first disappearance captured national attention in South Africa.
COURTESY *EVENING POST*, PORT ELIZABETH

Komodo Dragons

THE BRITISH Admiralty Pilot book covering Indonesian waters, still warns the modern seafarer to beware of the large and fearsome lizards that abound on the tiny island of Komodo. It was as recently as 1910 that a Dutch Colonial officer

An extract from the brochure publicising Simon's film.

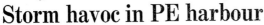

Storm havoc in PE harbour

Fishing boat Irene sinks

By COLIN URQUHART

A BHP in the Port Elizabeth harbour ran aground, another parted moorings, a fishing boat sank and many others were badly damaged during Saturday night's storm.

A gale of 50 knots also brought down the Port Office's VHF radio mast on Bethe's Hill at Chelsea and rain put the wind recorder at the airport out of action.

Wrecks, debris and mud brought down by the flooding Baakens River choked various parts of the harbour.

Afloat 2km yesterday the moorings of the Melloe, a 12 044 ton general cargo ship at No 1 berth, parted, causing the ship to drift away from the quay.

Its alerted his crew, who dropped an anchor and radioed port authorities for help.

While waiting for tugs to come to his aid the remaining two sterns moorings parted and the ship slowly drifted out into the basin.

"After clearing away moorings, which may have become entangled in the propellers, the main engines were started and we headed up into the wind in the direction of town," he said.

"But we gradually drifted about 245 metres across the harbour and on the mud bank in the corner between the Charl Malan Quay and No 2 quay. We were not more than about 45 metres from the swimming wall," Capt Rympers said.

Capt Rympers said the harbour tugs, Kabus Leshier and P. J. C. du Plessis, each about 11 hours to come to his aid,

and dock workers were able to attach new lines before she had drifted more than about 25 metres from the quayside.

The Adrena Son had to drop her anchor to stop her drifting into the harbour.

A spokesman for the Port Captain said yesterday it took about an hour to come cover the the two tugs.

He said all tug crews were off duty and some had to be called to town as far as the Western suburbs.

He said that in the circumstances the crew did very well in bringing the ships in 11 hours.

The Port Elizabeth fishing catamarans, Irene, which was moored at the repair jetty for about a year, parted moorings and was slanted to pieces as the rocks in the small boat harbour.

Pieces from the boat were strewn over a wide

damaged and bulkheads dented. The Verya?N's below she had battered and the Frai Lane's meal was broken.

Fishing boats moored along the Dom Pedro jetty appeared to escape the fury of the storm.

Most skippers reported little or no damage.

Yachts and fishing boats moored in the small boat harbour were not affected.

The Transmissions Engineer for the Post Office in Port Elizabeth, Mr N. W. Withers, said the 45-metre high VHF radio mast was blown over early yesterday.

He said technicians and workers were yesterday erecting a temporary mast and he hoped to have the VHF service operating by today.

Other radio channels were not affected.

A spokesman at the weather office at H. F. Verwoerd Airport, said the wind recorder was "put on the blink" after

part in the storm. An a? at which drifted across Port Elizabeth harbour after breaking her moorings, on Saturday night.

The African Sun (top) a swung out from the quay after breaking moorings.

Left: Flimsly tied up No 1 and No 3 berths 1 Port Elizabeth harbor are the African Sun (left) and the Mellos.

Both ships parted mooring during the weekend storm and the Mellos drifted about 245 metres across the harbour between two bittersweet. before littoral on the retaining ya (arrowed) before berthing as a residuum.

She was towed off by jew harbour tugs yesterday.

THE IRENE, the Port Elizabeth fishing boat which sank during the storm.

Alleged escaper held

HERALD CORRESPONDENT

PEARSTON — A Post sigen prisoner, with allegedly escaped from Somerset East on April 1: was captured on Frid: night on Karoo Peer farm of Mr Jack Darron port,

Gale, floods lash coast

Hundreds quit their homes

HERALD REPORTERS

HUNDREDS of people were forced to leave their homes, Port Elizabeth faced a water crisis, and the lower Gamtoos River valley became a potential flood-plain after the cyclone-type gale which brought drenching rains to the Eastern Cape coast on Saturday night.

In Decembrie, about 55 houses were flooded and

a storm, a Port Elizabeth floodplain crept upcourt die—

consisting of two pieces of steel and the oil concrete, broke in 4 places.

A 12 - kilometre section of the steel pipe was snapped near Humansde The concrete pipeline was undamaged and cross a section closer to Port Elizabeth allowed water from the concrete pipe refill the steel pipe.

Pylons

But two pontoons wrecked at the Van Stden River when ti pylons carrying the across the river we washed away by the waters.

Mr McCullum said decision would be take late yesterday as to whether impose water restriction The decision would furt depend on talks with the Mayor, Ben Bessemer, MPC, a the chairman of t Works Committee, Mr L. M. Bullin.

"If it is at all possible would be avoid rigid a trictions," said Mr McCe ham.

The Churchill Dam is also about half of Po

The final tempest: the storm that ravaged the Tsitsikamma forest when Simon was in the area in May 1977.

No 7834

Evening Post

Registered at the GPO as a
CITY LATE
Price 10c

WEDNESDAY, SEPTEMBER 14, 1977

Wow! Now it's R1050 to be won · See Page 2

U.S. JOINS WORLD PROTESTS

Biko seen as victim of apartheid

Sapa-Reuter-AP

WASHINGTON. — The United States Government has condemned the South African apartheid system for the death of the prominent Black leader, Mr Steve Biko, and called for a full investigation into the circumstances of his death.

The US statement is part of world-wide reaction to the announcement that Mr Biko died on Monday night in Pretoria while being detained by the Security Police.

Mr Biko, 30, was honorary president of the Black People's convention.

The US State Department said Mr Biko was "another victim of the apartheid system and the South African security legislation which supports that system."

The US was shocked and saddened by Mr Biko's death, and the statement. It added that a full investigation was called for.

Particular concern was expressed at the fact that Mr Biko died without either his family or attorney being notified of any deterioration in his health.

REPRESSION

The chairman of the US Senate Foreign Relations Committee on Africa, Senator Dick Clark, said the record of detainee detention in South Africa was "deeply disturbing."

He said Mr Biko's death was a hopeful sign to South Africans blocks but to all the people of the country who believed there was still a chance for a peaceful racial accommodation.

In London, the non-governmental international bodies' rights movement, Amnesty International, urged an immediate, open and independent inquiry into Mr Biko's death.

The movement sent a telegram to the Minister of Justice, Mr A.Z. Kruger, in which it said it was deeply concerned at Mr Biko's death while being "detained incommunicado under the South African security Police."

MARTYRS

The movement also wanted to know why Mr Biko had been "continually harassed by the South African police and repeatedly detained without trial."

Amnesty International said that whatever the cause of Mr Biko's death, "the responsibility rests with Mr Vorster and his Fascist police".

The Anti - Apartheid Movement said in London the "murder" of Mr Biko by the South African Police would shock the world. Mr Biko had joined the long list of martyrs who have died for the cause of freedom in South Africa.

Widespread grief and concern have been expressed throughout South Africa at Mr Biko's death. Political and religious leaders have attacked the Government for the police action taken against Mr Biko.

The president of the Southern African Catholic Bishops' Conference, said:

Mrs DIMNE HOLMES A'COURT and Mr TIM LIVERSEDGE are joining the search for her son.

MOTHER IN SEARCH FOR SON

A small, energetic woman from Australia flew into Port Elizabeth today to help step up the search for her son, whose disappearance has baffled police in two countries for three months.

Mrs Dilmne Holmes 'Court' was on her way to search for her son, a Stormes River, where a gut truck belonging to her son, Simon, 20, was found abandoned on a dusty forest path at the end of the Bloukrans Pass on June 9.

No one knows how it is there, why the motor plates, Bussiness chassis and engine numbers are removed or when it appeared to Mrs Holmes 'Court, who was at Oni when the truck left to Guavango Swimage in between on May 5.

Extensive police inquiries throughout South Africa and in Botswana have failed to uncover a trace of him since that time.

Publicity

With Mrs Holmes 'Court today was Mr Tim Liverage, a close friend of Simon (they are both sculptors and wildlife artist) who lives about 100 kilometres from him in Stormes. He has been searching for the past three weeks.

What Mrs Holmes 'Court hopes to do primarily by coming to South Africa is to draw as much publicity to the mystery of Simon subject to help to understand and from unlikely sources.

"The more widely it is publicised the more likelihood there is of someone using forward," she said.

"We are going down Stormes River to ...

● Please turn to Page 6, Col 4

Inside

TV Tonight 4
Diary 4
Crossword 6
TV Review 2
Radio Programmes 11
Teenage Crossword 11

The world's largest conventional ore carrier, Sishen, is in Algoa Bay on her first voyage from the Japanese shipyard to Saldanha where she will load her first cargo — ore for Japan.

Sishen, by far the largest ship in the South African register, cost her maiden trip rather. She will operate between the ore ports ferrying an average of 6½ shipments of ore a year. Each round voyage will take 55 days.

She has a carrying capacity of 169 878 tons, is 299 metres long with a draught of 17 metres and her service speed is 15½ knots.

She is in Algoa Bay, loafing her time to move on to Saldanha, because the document both her ore phenomenal speed. Her maiden trip held on January 12 this year, she was delivered on April 11 and she was delivered

more than a month ahead of schedule.

After completing trials off Japan she sailed to Algoa Bay because this is considered a safe anchorage — place where ships can be transferred where her crew can undergo familiarisation exercises.

She has been here about 10 days and will leave on October 4 or 5 for Cape Town, and for Saldanha on October 12 and 16 and still for Japan on October 13.

Kruger: there was no neglect

HUNGER STRIKE A 'RIGHT'

PRETORIA. — The Government was prepared for a propaganda onslaught following the death in detention of the banned Black leader, Mr Steve Biko, the Minister of Police and of Prisons, Mr J. T. Kruger, said here today.

Men held after theft

Police last night arrested two White men following a theft from a Port Elizabeth Wimpy Bar on September 6.

One of the men was arrested in Port Elizabeth and the other in East London.

The burglars gained entry to the Wimpy Bar through a front window.

They stole about R1 700 in cash from the safe and till, and took goods valued at R1500.

Oom Danie says

Rightful

Mr Kruger said the Security Police knew that if they had done anything wrong, he would be the first to take them to task.

He told the Transvaal National Party congress that it approved of this, and that everything had been done for Mr Biko that should have been done.

There had been a storm in Opposition newspapers over Mr Biko's death before the results of the post-mortem were known.

The English language Press had long predicted that if Mr Steve Biko or others are touched, all the propaganda machinery against South Africa will be instituted. We accept that.

2 HELD AFTER E CAPE MURDER

GRAAFF - REINET. — Two men, a Coloured and an African, have been arrested in connection with the murder of Mrs M. C. Ela, 84, of 1 Queen Street, Graaff-Reinet.

Mrs Ela was found dead in her sitting room on Saturday night by a neighbour. She had been battered and strangled to death.

Major J. J. Bensho, District Commandant of Police, at Graaff-Reinet, confirmed the arrests this afternoon but would not say any other that the arrests appear in court.

The funeral of Mrs Ela will take place from the NG Kerk in Graaff-Reinet at 3pm tomorrow.

Leon will be at function

An elderly woman from Australia flew into Port Elizabeth today...

The leader of the Labour Party of South Africa, Mr Sonny Leon, and the deputy chairman of the party's national executive, Mr Norman Middleton, will be guests of honour at a function in the Feather Market Hall on Friday to celebrate the party's successes in the recent Port Elizabeth Coloured Management Committee election.

12 held after break-ins

Police in the Cape Midlands Division have arrested 12 people in the past 24 hours in connection with 29 cases of housebreaking.

This was disclosed by the Divisional Criminal Investigation Officer, and Marcus van der Merwe.

Weather Forecast
Mild, changing
Page 2, col 9

ATTACK ON EAST CAPE COUPLE

An elderly Jeffreys Bay couple were treated at the Humansdorp Hospital and discharged, after being attacked in their home last night.

They are Mr Y. L. du Preez, 74, and his wife, Mrs Esther du Preez, 73.

At 10.30pm Mr Du Preez heard a noise in the house and went to investigate. In the passage he was attacked by a Coloured man who hit her on the head, injuring her mouth and cheek, and breaking her tooth.

Mr Du Preez was awakened by the noise and went to his wife's aid.

The intruder then attacked Mr Du Preez, injuring his head and hand. According to the police, nothing appears to have been stolen from the house.

QUOTE

STEVE BIKO was a man of wisdom, honesty, peace and humanity. His death is draining will strengthen the determination of all those working for a free and just South Africa both inside and outside the country.

— The British chairmen of Amnesty International, The Rev Paul Oestreicher, is a clergyman in London.

Ethnée arrives in South Africa to search for Simon just as the country is plunged into a political crisis with the death of Steve Biko.
COURTESY *EVENING POST*, PORT ELIZABETH

Police baffled over sculptor

24 AUG 1977
HERALD CORRESPONDENT

JOHANNESBURG. — South African Police are baffled by the disappearance of a wild life sculptor from the Okavango Swamps in Botswana who came to South Africa on a seven-day visit.

The sculptor — Simon Holmes - A - Court, 38, has not been seen since he crossed the border into South Africa on May 5.

The only clue to his disappearance is the sculptor's Datsun bakkie — found abandoned on a lonely forest path near the Storms River in the Eastern Cape on June 9.

clothes and briefcase, however, were missing.

Neither police nor Mr Holmes - A - Court's friend, Mr Tim Livetsedge, who has come from Botswana to join the search, can find a motive for his disappearance.

For the past two years Mr Holmes - A - Court has been engaged in wild life sculpture, working from his little cottage in Maun on the edge of the Okavango Swamps.

Cottage

But according to Mr Liversedge his sculptor friend never returned to the cottage since he entered South Africa on a seven - day visitor's

E Cape police seek sculptor

27 AUG 1977

By KEITH ROSS

Mystery still surrounds the disappearance of the Botswana sculptor, Simon Holmes-A-Court, 38, whose pickup van was found abandoned near Storms River.

The District Criminal Investigation Officer for

Sculptor case baffles police

30 AUG 1977

By JOHAN SWANEPOEL

BAFFLED police who are trying to find the Botswana sculptor, Mr Simon Holmes - a'Court, 38, are anxious to establish how and when he came into South Africa, if at all.

His Datsun pickup was found abandoned near the eastern end of the Bloukrans Pass on June 9. It was hidden behind some trees about 200 metres from the main road on a lonely path leading from

---

Missing man's mother joins hunt

15 SEP 1977
HERALD REPORTER

THE mother of the missing wanderer, Mr Simon Holmes a'Court left Port Elizabeth with police yesterday for the Bloukrans Pass site where his pickup was found abandoned more than three months ago.

He was last heard of more than four months ago when he entered South Africa from Botswana at Koopfontein border post, Western Transvaal, on May When his pickup was found it had been abandoned for some time.

The licence and insurance discs as well as the number plates were missing. So were his clothes and briefcase. The engine and chassis numbers had been scratched out.

His mother, Mrs Ethne Holmes ia'Court, who left her home near Perth, Australia, at the weekend, flew to Port Elizabeth from Johannesburg yesterday morning, confident that her son was still alive. "I would not be here if I did not believe this."

She was accompanied by a friend of her son, Mr

Verwoerd Airport by Lt W. Benn and Const. J. Cloete of the Uitenhage CID.

In an interview from Storms River, last night, Mrs Holmes a'Court said she had taken possession of her son's pickup. Today she would visit the spot where it was found and interview the forest rangers who discovered it.

She intended returning to Port Elizabeth tomorrow.

their stay in the Storms River area to arrange for the pickup standing at the police station to be taken to Johannesburg and to get the atmosphere of the place.

"It is the type of place which would have attracted him. He may be wandering around there doing his own thing."

However, she found his absence of more than four months perturbing. She thought it possible that he might be suffering from loss of memory.

"Mr Liversedge did not rule out the possibility that his friend had been murdered.

"But this is one of a number of possibilities. He

may be wandering around in the forests somewhere, or he could have boarded a yacht. He has done both before," he said.

He and Mrs Holmes a'Court held discussions with Brig P. J. Hugo, Divisional Commissioner of Police, before leaving for Storms River, accompanied by Lt Benn.

COURTESY *EVENING POST*, PORT ELIZABETH

The Vark River bridge, a few hundred metres
from where Simon's remains were found.
AUTHOR'S PRIVATE COLLECTION

The Matlapaneng Bridge in Maun that featured in Bodo Muche's nightmare.
PHOTO COURTESY TIM AND JUNE LIVERSEDGE

Simon's Datsun was found abandoned on the South African Coast.

Lorenda Savage, who made the grisly discovery of Simon's remains in 1980.

Daphne in 2000.
PHOTO COURTESY DAPHNE HILDEBRANDT

Ethnée Holmes à Court on the Heytesbury stud in 2000.
AUTHOR'S PRIVATE COLLECTION

wide-lapelled fawn jacket, was a trained pilot and was waiting to meet her having flown himself down from Maun. They headed to a hotel and plotted what would be a frenetic ten days of travel around southern Africa. Both Liversedge and Ethnée had agreed on one thing: despite the omens and any conspiracy theories thrown up by the strange state in which Simon's car was found, they were both sure Simon, a man of great resilience, strength and independence, was still alive.

The next day, less than forty-eight hours after Biko's death, Ethnée and Liversedge flew into Port Elizabeth, a town still reeling from shock and coming to grips with a police force that had, in part, been responsible for the death. When the determined 61-year-old mother and grandmother arrived on a paradoxically mild Wednesday, 14 September—more than four months since Simon was last seen—a journalist asked her if she felt her son was still alive and she snapped, 'I wouldn't be here if I didn't believe him to be alive.'

Ethnée was pictured wearing a suede jacket (bought on a trip to San Francisco) with a buttoned-up floral shirt and her thick black hair swept back. She stared imperiously at the press contingent through large oval sunglasses. It looked like a star from the silver screen had just pulled into town.

Ethnée and Liversedge made that day's late edition of Port Elizabeth's *Evening Post,* sharing the front page under banner headlines about the death of Biko, which read: 'US JOINS WORLD PROTESTS: Biko seen as a victim of apartheid'.

At the airport Ethnée and Liversedge were met by Lieutenant Benn and Constable Cloete, colleagues of the men who decades later would seek amnesty for their involvement in Biko's death. This extraordinary confluence of events makes the tale of Holmes à Court's disappearance, and his presence in the Eastern Cape as the resistance efforts escalated, all the more intriguing in light of evidence that has emerged since.

The police were pessimistic about the missing sculptor and their musings with journalists carried a sinister tone. Divisional commander Brigadier Hugo was already openly contemplating Ethnée's worst fears when he told journalists of police efforts to search the area: 'You can walk over a corpse in the Tsitsikamma forests without knowing it is there.'

Simon had kept his clandestine activities quiet, as you would expect, but he had told at least four people close to him, including Ethnée and Daphne, that he had been involved in espionage. He had never revealed it to Liversedge or Muche. But if Holmes à Court was working undercover as an agent for the forces of apartheid, the chance that he was still alive looked slim.

The scenarios haunted Ethnée. Maybe Simon had made contact again with his agency colleagues after his trip around the world and was back on the payroll? Heaven forbid, perhaps he was implicated in the death of Steve Biko somehow? Maybe the discovery of the Datsun by the Eastern Cape police landed them with an investigation they never had a hope of solving if the mysterious third force of South Africa's security agencies were involved. Ethnée never discussed this aspect of Simon's life publicly, instead preferring to make discreet inquires via the embassies and diplomatic channels. But no one knew a thing, or at least that's what they told her. So decentralised was the chain of command in South Africa's feared security apparatus that this was hardly surprising.

On 14 September Ethnée put on a brave face, inspired by Liversedge's confidence that her son was still alive, and was stoical at her Port Elizabeth press conference.

Simon has been out of touch with his friends and family for long periods before, but I must admit not as long as this.

The more widely it is publicised the more likelihood there is of someone coming forward. The fact that he had disappeared was no surprise to anyone, he has done this sort of thing before.

I decided to come myself because up to now our friends in this country, the police and especially Mr Liversedge, have done all they possibly can to find Simon. It is time I did something as well.

We are going down to see the truck, which will then be railed to Johannesburg. We will spend two nights there and look around the area and see if we can talk to the various locals and just get the atmosphere of the place.

Forests attracted him, and I think everybody felt there was nothing to worry about when he disappeared and there was a considerable silence—until his truck was found. Then Mr Liversedge contacted me and asked if I had had any word from Simon. Since then I have been on the telephone every day— calling friends and colleagues in Cape Town, Johannesburg, Botswana, the police and the embassies.

I don't know why he was in South Africa because he did not tell us, and I don't think he told anybody except to say he was coming to Johannesburg for some materials for his bronze casting.

For the next two days Ethnée and Liversedge toured the Storm's River area and detectives took them to the spot where the beige two-door Datsun 620 *bakkie* had been found. *Bakkie* is the popular South African description, derived from Afrikaans, for a ute or pick-up truck.

Ethnée and Tim discussed whether, in heading down to Storm's River, Simon had intended to visit the nearby Knysna forest where elephants were still thought to roam, or maybe the Addo National Park, an elephant sanctuary. He might have stopped in the forest, Ethnée reasoned, to look around and while he was taking a walk his pick-up could have been stolen.

The police showed Ethnée how the Datsun had been driven down a forest track and hidden among thick bush. The area was a lovely picnic spot, a small open park surrounded by a grove of trees with forest trails leading off in several directions and the Tsitsikamma ranges rising just a couple of kilometres away to the north. Ethnée was overwhelmed by the beauty of the place. She told Liversedge: 'It is the sort of area that would attract him. It is a very lonely, wild spot, very quiet and very beautiful. I feel he could still be here.'

Tsitsikamma is derived from the language of the Khoikhoi, and is a combination of *tse-tsesa*, or clear, and *gami*, meaning water. The Khoikhoi were a nomadic people who inhabited south-western South Africa when the seventeenth-century European settlers landed at the Cape.

The area enchants visitors with its evergreen forests of yellow-wood trees, some more than eight hundred years old and reaching a height of sixty metres. The Tsitsikamma and the Cape boast the highest plant concentration in the world, with more than one thousand per square kilometre. There is still the odd leopard.

A dense temperate zone, rivers and creeks sourced from the Tsitsikamma mountains, which rise steeply from the coast, feed the forests all year around. It's a growth cycle forest, where gaps on the cool sun-dappled forest floor allow space for new trees to grow. The forest sings sweetly with bubbling brooks and the calls of a carnivalesque array of birdlife, red and emerald green feathers backlit by the sun filtering through the forest canopy.

The forests sweep down to a rugged coastline, characterised by enormous boulders and huge surf. Storm's River is deep, wide and cool, and it bends its way out of a gorge to meet a surging Indian Ocean where wild waves whip up lathers of foam. Just to the north lies Jeffrey's Bay, now one of the most favoured destinations for surfers from around the world. Since the sixties travelling surfers have made their pilgrimage here, where wave after wave hits the headland to slide diagonally down the coast for nearly a kilometre. This powerful and sensual landscape is a long way from Maun but, like the swamplands that Maun fringes, is just as beautiful.

Khoikhoi, or Hottentots as South Africans call them, means 'men of men'. They hunted with bows and arrows and lived in transportable beehive huts in the Tsitsikamma. But the culture and tribes have been all but wiped out thanks to invasions from both the Zulus and the Europeans.

The forests where Simon disappeared have echoed with the pain of human sacrifice for centuries. The Zulus, under their King Dingaan, the successor to the famous Shaka, conducted one of their raids on the trekking Boers, the Dutch settlers and the generation from which apartheid was born, in this area. The Boers were on their 'Great Trek' north, a pilgrimage to hoped-for promised lands and a historical symbol that explains much of the Afrikaner psyche in their belief that they too have sacrificed their blood to South African soil. The *voortrekkers* had headed north after disputes with the British and their rule in the Cape colony. These deeply conservative folk, using the bible as their guide—as travellers today would use the *Lonely Planet*—met fierce resistance from the Zulus. The Bloukrans massacre, in almost the same spot that Simon disappeared, was one of a series of bloody battles with Zulus. But in the Tsitsikamma now, the cries of Zulus descending on the trekkers brandishing their assegais is hard to imagine—it remains a peaceful place.

Storm's River lies just north of the smaller Vark River. Both run through the Tsitsikamma forest and are a central attraction of the colourful Garden Route, running all the way to Cape Town, about 700 kilometres to the west.

The Botswana border crossing was about a day's drive away, which meant if Simon drove straight to the spot he was likely to have been in the Storm's River area on 6 May, a Friday. While in Perth, Ethnée had telephoned Simon's friends along the route between Maun and Johannesburg. He had not stayed with any of them since 5 May.

The evidence suggested that Simon had just kept driving— alone. The speculation that he may have been kidnapped and forced to drive that far south, or that he was already dead and then his captors dumped his body in the forest, was ruled out.

In a breakthrough in the investigation, police found two petrol attendants at Humansdorp, a village near Jeffrey's Bay about ninety kilometres away from where his car was found, who remembered Simon.

They told police they remembered Simon filling up with petrol at Humansdorp, which tallies with the evidence police found in the car—two cans full of petrol in the back and the petrol tank itself three-quarters full. Ethnée quizzed the police on this point, questioning why, or indeed how, Simon would have extra fuel in jerry cans when there was petrol rationing in South Africa at the time. But the police said the attendants swore they sold Simon the petrol.

So what had happened in that ninety-minute drive west from Humansdorp along the N2 highway as it wove its way between the rugged Indian Ocean coastline and the magnificient blue-purple Tsitsikamma ranges? Was it somewhere along that highway that Simon made a secret rendezvous? For instance, did he meet an agent as part of some secret service plot? Was it somewhere along that route that Simon found himself involved in something that was way over his head?

An intense media campaign, which included photos of Simon, published in the newspapers throughout South Africa over August and early September, and regular radio reports, yielded no clues. Against Ethnée's hopes no witnesses had come forward. It was then that Ethnée decided to contact Africa's mysterious world of the occult and witchcraft to try to find her son.

The story of the missing man was being lost in the maelstrom. The country was in the grip of political upheaval, and attention and resources were directed elsewhere—not least to the institution of apartheid, which the police force was playing its part in trying to uphold. The world was aghast at South Africa's racial policies and sanctions loomed. CBS television's legendary Walter Cronkite asked then British foreign secretary David Owen: 'What can the world do about South Africa's racial policies?' Owen replied, 'This is where you find yourself up against granite when you speak to Mr Vorster.' John Vorster was the prime minister of South Africa at the time.

Against these extraordinary events unfolding in the country of her birth, Ethnée was growing despondent. In the end, Robert's commitment to Liversedge that he would employ an army to find Simon came to naught as the crushing reality started bearing down on everyone concerned. Simon had vanished. Ethnée was no fool—the police force had all but given up on her son and left him for dead. She and Liversedge took charge of Simon's Datsun, and Liversedge drove it to Port Elizabeth where it was then railed back to Johannesburg.

Ethnée had always been one to dabble in spirituality and the occult and would often say she could hear her mother's voice in her head. Ethnée would always say how her mother was 'fey', a traditional term for a clairvoyant or someone who has contact with the spiritual world: 'I remember when she was dying I was with her and she said to me if I can come back I will come back.' She decided Liversedge should help her find Africa's most powerful sangoma—a holy man or woman said to be able to divine the spirits. The sangoma is a tradition of the Zulu and Ndebele people. Using their implements—

usually a collection of bones, pebbles and dice—the sangoma channels ancestral spirits and deceased loved ones to offer guidance. If it worked, Ethnée would surely find her son.

As Liversedge set about finding a sangoma, Ethnée, exhausted, flew to Durban to see an old friend, Peggy Whittaker, to try to regain some strength. Liversedge flew to Johannesburg. He knew some people there who might be able to help in his search for a sangoma. He had been given the number of a woman who, surprisingly, lived in the exclusive suburb of Houghton. It was not the kind of suburb one would normally associate with witchdoctors in Africa. Houghton boasts tree-lined avenues and huge houses surrounded by high security fences and patrolled by drooling German shepherds and Rottweilers. But Liversedge was assured the woman—a wealthy white South African—was training to be a sangoma and had powerful teachers.

Liversedge arrived at the address in Houghton and the mysterious woman greeted him. She could have been a suburban housewife but she assured Liversedge she had made contact with her principal teachers, traditional healers from a village outside of Johannesburg, and they were prepared to help.

Ethnée flew back into town the next day and Liversedge briefed her with the plan. They would have to drive to the outskirts of the city late that night and wait for two black gentlemen to arrive in a car.

It was a clear, crisp Johannesburg night and, at the appointed time, a car approached. There was a prearranged flash of lights which was the signal. The two men, wearing suits and carrying expensive leather briefcases, hopped out, approached Ethnée and Liversedge, and jumped into the back seat. All four were jumpy. The two men were cautious and hid below the window line in the back seat—this was South Africa under apartheid, after all and the reason for such a clandestine approach. Ethnée and Liversedge were nervous too, wondering if the men could be trusted. One spoke, giving another address back in Houghton. 'We will meet with the woman again there.'

The four drove back to the century-old mansion in Houghton. The woman welcomed them and ushered them into a wood panelled library with wall-to-wall books and expensive Persian carpets on the floor. In the middle of the room there was a mattress, and all four were asked to take off their shoes. The two men in suits started questioning Ethnée and Liversedge, asking about Simon. Suddenly one opened his briefcase and produced a bag of bones.

Liversedge had noticed that a big heavy door into the room, about four metres high, was slightly ajar and felt there was somebody behind it, listening to them.

The bones were thrown onto the floor. The door creaked and moved slightly. To Liversedge's amazement a black cat walked in—it appeared to have pushed the door itself—and stealthily crossed the floor to where they were seated. It sniffed each bone while everyone sat in silence.

One of the men started muttering. His voice became clearer, telling Ethnée he could visualise Simon and said he could see him with a woman with long dark hair. Liversedge immediately took that as a reference to Daphne. 'I can see pain in one hand and I can see mountains. He is still alive and he is in that direction, near the forest. Near the sea.' He walked to the window and pointed again. Liversedge could tell he was pointing south—the direction of the Tsitsikamma forest. Ethnée and Liversedge were shaken by the revelations and didn't feel as though the men were duping them. The reference to Simon's hand was intriguing—he had once been bitten by a snake. Before Ethnée and Liversedge left, the men said Ethnée would have more news in three weeks—the middle of October.

But any hope would soon begin to fade. 'It was horribly creepy and the house was creepy,' Ethnée would later say. 'We all sat on the floor but I think they were a dead loss. They said I would know in three weeks. Well three weeks came and went and we still didn't know.'

The next day, 17 September, Ethnée, in despair that little was coming of her journey, flew with Liversedge in his single engine plane from Johannesburg to Maun, about 830 kilometres to the north-west. The route took Ethnée over a vast, sparsely vegetated plain that makes up the south-eastern corner of Botswana before the Kalahari Desert looms on the left and then later, closer to Maun, the enormous Makgadikgadi saltpans shimmer a brilliant white below.

In September 1977, Maun would only bring Ethnée heartache. After her arrival that day she met with Daphne for the first time and there were 'floods of tears' as they discussed Simon. Ethnée did not stay long, just a couple of days, as she set about finalising Simon's affairs in Maun—a desperately difficult thing for a mother to do when she is clinging to the hope that her son is still alive.

Ethnée visited Simon's shack and the contrast with life back in Perth on Robert's horse stud was, again, a source of bewilderment for Ethnée. A simple grass hut ten kilometres out of town was Simon's home, and where it seemed he was perfectly happy. It was a simple reed hut, just like the ones the local tribes, the Batawana people, used. Its one concession to modernity was a concrete floor and electricity, but it still boasted a circular mud wall reinforced with straight wooden poles cut from saplings. A thatched conical roof topped it. On the other great southern continent to the east, Simon's brother Robert was driving expensive imported cars like Porsches and Mercedes and had a growing family, living in Perth's wealthy beachside suburb of Cottesloe among other lawyers and well-to-do types. These two brothers lived life at opposite ends of the social spectrum.

Despite Simon's minimalism he had left something behind. When Ethnée and Liversedge went to his hut it was just as he had left it. Prominent was a workbench and on it was a completed plasticine model of a large elephant, standing nearly half a metre tall. Ethnée and his friends would come to regard this piece as Simon's best work. 'It was so accurate and so lifelike, he could have made his name as a sculptor on that piece alone,' Liversedge would later say.

Elephants had always fascinated Simon, his mother describing how he once performed a Caesarean on a dying elephant in the futile attempt to save its baby. Perhaps Simon identified with these gentle and noble creatures, the silent ones that lope along casually with a curiously elastic gait. Simon used to spend hours observing them.

For Ethnée, it was too much to bear. It was 22 September. It had been a whirlwind tour lasting just ten days and had cost about AUS$10 000. She bade farewell to Maun and started her journey home, heartbroken.

Daphne would later write to friends describing her time with Simon, tragedy and time softening her account of how things had ended with Simon:

I loved Simon very dearly. To me he was everything I ever wanted. He loved the wild outdoors and had such a great affinity with the ways of the bush but never boasted of what he knew. So much came totally as a sixth sense to him. We spent many happy hours in this newly found attraction for each other. We ran around on soft white sandbanks on river islands, chasing each other in bright moonlight. We used to don goggles and swim between great weed beds, holding hands as we floated or dropped between the swaying colours of plant life. An inflated tyre tube gave us the perfect bench from which to sit and survey the fading light from the river's edge while watching flocks of egrets flying home to roost. Yes, sadness was all that followed. I had been to Tsitsikamma forests too, to the beaches before and after, always thinking I would see a face that would tell me everything. Amongst crowds, through fern walkways, alone on a bench— would I not find or see a familiar face? Never.

Liversedge could not give up on his old friend. He wondered if Simon was trying to stay low from his family, from Daphne, or someone else. He continued to contact friends, trying to work out where he might be. Then, just weeks after Ethnée had left, there was a breakthrough. Tony Challis called Liversedge with a lead.

Challis, like a lot of men in Maun, was in the hunting game. But he loved the sea, which was a problem if you lived in landlocked Botswana. Challis had bought a property near Storm's River just kilometres away from where Simon disappeared. He had been away and just heard about Simon. He had some startling news.

'The night before Simon left we were having a chat in town,' Challis told Liversedge. 'I was telling him about my place on the Tsitsikamma coast. He sounded really interested, things didn't seem to be going so well with Daphne.

'It's way down the end of a track. There's a little thatched cottage. It's a two-room place that overlooks the sea. I said to Simon you can go and live there as long as you want, it's an excellent place to sit quietly and sculpt your animals . . . and no one will know you're there, you can have it as long as you want.'

Challis told Simon he hadn't been there for over a year and it might need some tender loving care but it would be an ideal retreat.

Liversedge rushed through the house to tell his wife June. 'When you consider where Tony's house is in relation to where his car was found—well, it's only ten kilometres or so,' he said. 'Simon's the sort of guy who lives easily off the sea, you could dive for shellfish and live comfortably there. Perhaps he has decided to go and opt out.'

Liversedge left the next day, alone. He knew if Simon was lying low the last thing he'd want was a posse coming down to find him. He had possession of Simon's car and decided to drive it back down, retracing Simon's steps. He told no one else, trusting no one and not wishing to raise expectations.

He stopped off at little trading stores and spoke to the petrol station attendants in Humansdorp who had remembered Simon's car. He was more and more excited the closer he got to Challis's shack, convinced he'd soon be sharing a cup of tea with Simon, hearing why he had decided to go to ground.

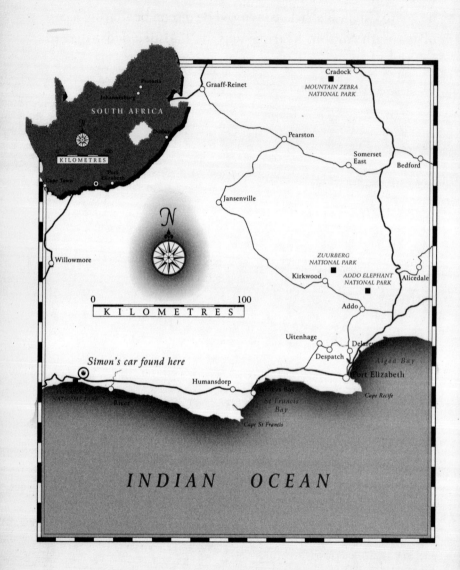

The Discovery

1977–80

But now I saw Death as near as I believe as I have never ever seen him. He was whispering from time to time in the rising wind.

Winston Churchill

As Simon drove towards the southern coast on Thursday 5 May 1977—the day he had left Maun—the weather started to turn. A powerful storm was brewing and it seemed to follow Simon, like a lion stalking its prey.

He arrived on Friday 6 May, having slept in his car overnight on the road down—there was no evidence he had stayed with anyone. He made the stop at Humansdorp for petrol and continued towards Challis's shack.

But over the Friday and Saturday the barometer would fall sharply. A freak weather pattern had formed. The South African weather bureau was reporting a strange confluence of events: a storm sandwiched between two high pressure systems was building into a massive hurricane. They get big blows in

Port Elizabeth, but nothing like this one. It was the final tempest, shadowing Simon's last hours. The storm swept in from the south-east, descended on Port Elizabeth and then, like Simon, took a path west, directly towards the Tsitsikamma forest.

Radio reports told residents to be on full alert. According to the Bureau of Meteorology: 'A high pressure area behind a cold front started moving east over the Atlantic Ocean. Soon afterwards a low pressure area over the Free State started moving south-east and it would normally have passed out over the sea. However, it was prevented from doing so by a high pressure area behind a hot humid air mass building up over the Indian Ocean. The two exceptionally high pressures converged over the Port Elizabeth area, trapping the exceptionally low pressure areas between them.'

As Simon arrived in the Tsitsikamma forest the weather closed in. On Saturday it hit hard. Hundreds of homes were flattened and communication and water supplies were cut. Ships were torn from their moorings at Port Elizabeth, like the 12 000-tonne general cargo ship the *Moliro*, which drifted across the harbour and was dumped on a mudbank 245 metres away. Another, *The Africa Sun*, lost its stern moorings and most of its bow moorings until the captain successfully fought the storm and was able to drop anchor. Smaller boats and yachts were smashed against rocks. At least seven people lost their lives.

Were Simon's last hours spent in the midst of this terrible blow?

Rounding a bend Liversedge caught sight of the shack. The area was every bit as beautiful as Challis had described but, oh, the despair. The shack was uninhabitable. The roof had collapsed. As Liversedge approached his spirits suddenly lifted when he heard movement inside. He crept up to a broken window and peered in. A cow, nonchalant and disinterested, looked back at him. He walked through a front portal, the door hanging askew. There was cow dung everywhere. Events seem to have conspired against Simon so terribly. It was a bitter blow.

Liversedge did not dwell in the Tsitsikamma long, desolate that again his search had ended so depressingly. There was no sign of Simon. He turned on his heel and jumped back into the Datsun. 'It's bloody useless,' he shouted, banging the steering wheel. He cranked over the Datsun and flattened the accelerator, tearing down the track and out onto the highway. He couldn't stop—driving through, all the way back to Maun.

For three more years there would be no news. Ethnée kept busy, helping Robert build up his horse stud, speaking less frequently to the police as the years slipped by and there was clearly nothing further to report. She asked Robert, with his now considerable financial resources, to investigate information into Simon's clandestine activities, but again nothing came of it. The people in Maun resumed their lives. Daphne and Bernie never reconciled their differences and were officially separated.

Then, on 11 February 1980, three girls from the Storm's River district went walking in the forest. Lorenda Savage, seventeen, and her two girlfriends Beryl Booysen, sixteen, and Bernadine Alexander, seventeen, headed into the forest from the nearby village carrying small knives to cut thin saplings and stems from the lush undergrowth. They used the material to make brooms. They had made their way down into the valley, called Bloukrans Gorge, and walked across a small bridge over the Vark River. An old harvesting track ran alongside the southern bank of the river and it afforded access upstream of the Vark, which was otherwise bordered by cliffs.

This section of the forest is quiet and bewitching. The rustle of bushes alerts the foraging bushbuck and bushpigs or, rarely, a leopard. Here the sun filters through to the forest floor and catches the Vark, which runs a ruby red. The tannins from the decaying fynbos (a kind of heather unique to the Cape region) in the Tsitsikamma mountains above sweep into the river and in the sunlight the water is scarlet. As the Vark River tumbles down over rocks and into deep pools, whitish rocks underneath on the shallow river bed are vaguely discernible; they are eerie, like pale pink lifeless human shapes. To be there is to be like God's sommelier holding Mother Nature to the eye only to catch glimpses of disturbing shapes lurking within the red glow of the river.

Lorenda, Beryl and Bernadine were part of the 'coloured' community working for the timber company—from the same group of workers who had found Simon's car three years earlier. Lorenda led Beryl and Bernadine down the river, weaving her way through the forest floor. She saw a patch rich with ferns and bent over to start collecting some brush. As she pushed apart the foliage, she screamed. She had come face to face with a skeleton.

She turned and ran towards her friends, yelling incoherently. They started screaming too, running out of the forest. They made it onto the bridge and saw two men coming down the road—Jaap Fick and Jim Swaart, who had been planning to spend the day fishing for eels in the Vark River. Lorenda, distraught, told them of her shocking discovery.

She pointed to the spot and the men made their way there while she and her friends waited at the bridge. Fick and Swaart stood over the skeleton, shaking their heads. They wandered back to the girls and they all made their way up the hill to tell the foresty manager, Pierre Theron.

For months afterwards, whenever Lorenda closed her eyes to sleep at night she saw the image of the skeleton. There were 'church shoes', as Lorenda called them—smart brown shoes you would only wear to church. Pieces of leg and foot bone were found sticking out of the shoes. There were also pieces of blue nylon windbreaker.

Theron remembered the case of the sculptor from Botswana and wondered immediately if the skeleton was his. He called the police at Storm's River and within an hour Theron, Swaart and Fick and the local constabulary were looking at the site. Investigating the crime scene they knew immediately the mystery behind the disappearance of Simon Holmes à Court might be solved.

Three

The Journalist

1995

If circumstances lead me, I will find
Where the truth is hid, though it were hid indeed
Within the centre

Hamlet, William Shakespeare

As Robert Holmes à Court's name leapt to prominence in Australia and on the international business stage, strangely there was always one thing missing from the dialogue: his brother. No one, it seemed, dared mention his name. For years it would be so.

But then a journalist found himself with time on his hands and a longing to travel to Africa. It was 1995. A year earlier the first all-race elections in South Africa had finally brought to power the world's most respected revolutionary, Nelson 'Madiba' Mandela, who immediately set about healing the nation's wounds. South Africa appeared to be on the cusp of a liberal democratic renaissance—for a freelance journalist it was the only place to be in the world.

Mike Carter was twenty-nine years old, an Australian from Perth and had spent years backpacking. He was the kind of man who fell in and out of love and meandered through a life of no commitment. He'd started out as a journalist in his home town and had written about Robert's rise and rise but had not given the family much thought in the five years he had been travelling the world, picking up work for various magazines and newspapers where he could.

His first day in South Africa did not start so smoothly. Carter flew in to Johannesburg from London. Johannesburg is the country's biggest city, sprawling across a vast, dry, elevated alluvial plain. It was once one of the world's biggest wealth generators, mostly lining the pockets of mining capitalists in London and South Africa. But the cheap black labour who worked so hard for a pittance in the city's gold mines has spawned an army of displaced youths who now lurked in the shadows of Johannesburg's skyscrapers. After dumping his luggage at a suburban B&B, and far too flippant about the dangers of the big city, Carter headed to a restaurant, ordered a pizza and necked a few beers. With these bottles of bravado digesting, he decided to walk into the city.

Before long he knew he had walked into something sinister. A dozen young men and some children—eyes glazed over from sniffing petrol and glue—whistled and gathered like a pack of hyenas around Carter, before baring their flickknives like fangs. They were at his throat. The younger ones went through his pockets and Carter winced as the cool blades pressed against a thumping pulse—they would draw blood at just the flex of a muscle. They took his cash and ran. It seems a spotter had alerted them to a police car because seconds later a yellow van of the force rounded the corner.

Carter ran towards it shouting, arms outstretched like a frantic toddler running to his mother. Two policemen hopped out, pulled their pistols in an empty show of force and spirited him into the back of the van. He was locked behind the wire mesh of the police van like a criminal. The police dropped him at the B&B with barely a word, just a faint smile playing at the corners of their mouths, looking at the shattered and humiliated *musungu* (white man). Welcome to Africa. Carter had had his first lesson on how Africa soon finds you out. Jut your chin and expect to be decked. In Africa death is always just a heartbeat away: life and death run together as easily as 'black and white'.

The hapless Carter had often found himself in scrapes like this. He didn't seem to learn much from them and hardly appeared to be the type to unravel a mystery. But it wouldn't be long before he was on the trail.

He only stayed a few more days in Johannesburg, and would only sheepishly venture out into the more rarefied environs of Sandton, the sanitised suburban shopping city to the north of the CBD, to catch a film. It was not quite the image he had of himself stirring up some big feature stories from the heart of Soweto, the largest black township from the days of apartheid.

Instead, bruised by his encounter, he decided to head to Cape Town. It was an appropriate enough destination. Cape Town's magnetism is the mountain: a 1000 metre flat-top rising above the crystal waters of Table Bay. It seems Cape Town is a rock of stability and shelter for sailors and land-bound travellers alike. In its shadows rests a port town vibrant with an extraordinary array of cultures, once frozen in isolation thanks to apartheid, now gradually thawing and running together. Cape Malays, English, Dutch, Zulu, Xhosa, Portuguese and Indian: all are represented, some more obviously than others. Zulus perform ritual dances for the tourists in the city's centre while others might find a quiet Portuguese restaurant tucked away in a sleepy corner. But like in his home town of Perth, Carter found that redolence of a British colonial past. Perth had its own prison island—Rottnest Island, off the coast, where convicts were incarcerated. Cape Town's Robben Island, however, once used by the British as a penal and a leper colony, was altogether more infamous, playing a central role in the National Party's apartheid machinery: it was where Mandela was locked away for nearly two decades.

Carter soon found his feet among the journalists and the printing presses of the *Cape Argus* newspaper. The newspaper offices are still located in the city centre, unlike the cost-conscious trend elsewhere in the world which has seen many journalists and the presses shifted to lower rent suburban areas away from their life force. The *Argus* is one of the few afternoon newspapers left in the world—Carter had started on one back in Perth and quickly slotted into the familiar early morning deadlines.

Many of the hundreds of thousands of workers who live in the impoverished Cape flats and travel to the city and back every day were avid readers of the *Argus*. It splashed sensational headlines and pitched its stories to appeal to the Cape's teeming underprivileged classes. In 1995 it led front page after front page with big brassy colour photographs of Princess Diana as the news broke that she and Prince Charles were to divorce.

Carter was roped into economics coverage. South Africa was feeling the flush of the huge foreign capital inflows amid investor excitement about its faltering democracy. Cape Town, always a favourite on the tourist circuit in any case, was hopping as new cafes and businesses popped up. Confidence was at an all-time high after years of political isolation, and it was kicked along by the republic's World Cup rugby victory that same year.

Carter was humbled among South African journalists. In that country simply to cover a municipal round meant you were risking your life. Chain-smoking reporters spoke of dodging bullets just to report on some local elections in Kwa-Zulu Natal. It was one of many anecdotes he heard about in the decades of flak-jacket journalism that so many of the local reporters had endured. There might have been criticism of some South African journalists for pandering to the white oppressors during the apartheid years, some of it undoubtedly justified, but Carter couldn't help but think if a country is willing to wear the international opprobrium of shutting out the foreign press corps, imagine the pressure brought to bear domestically. On every drag of a reporter's cigarette there was often urgency, as though it would be their last. They were a tough lot. It was a common trait of Africans, of all hues. They are tough and fiercely independent.

One afternoon after deadline, Carter met Hugh Roberton, the chief political correspondent for the *Argus*. He had travelled the world, including a stint as a correspondent in New York, racking up more than thirty years of journalistic experience. Dressed immaculately, he was South African but sported a crisp accent that was difficult to place, a true 'internationalist' you find on many an editorial floor. Carter's accent had attracted some interest there as well: most South African journalists and editors were leaving to go to Australia—not many came the other way. When the conversation turned to where Carter had lived and worked as a journalist, Roberton asked if he had covered the Holmes à Courts. Yes, he said, he had followed Robert.

'I knew him and his brother Simon,' Roberton said.

'His brother? I didn't even know he had a brother. Are you sure? I followed the Holmes à Courts quite a bit and I've never heard about a brother,' said Carter.

'I went to school with both of them. It's the strangest story about Simon. He disappeared. No one knows what happened to him.'

Carter was intrigued. Roberton said that after leaving school he had lost contact with Simon over the years, and had been shocked to read in his own newspaper in 1977 that he was missing. He told Carter to check the files at the *Argus*—some of the newsclips might still be there.

Carter wandered into the *Argus* library, dominated by rows and rows of grey filing cabinets. Within them was stored South Africa's tortured history—millions of newspaper clippings. Months could be spent reading through the day-to-day cycle of news in a country with such a turbulent history, Carter thought. The recorded minutiae as the government went about its vile experiment in social engineering should be mandatory reading for students. It was so absurd. Like how many blacks had been reclassified coloureds, coloured reclassified black, no one reclassified as white. Disturbing snapshots in time all dutifully presented in yellowing manila folders. The trial and internment of Nelson Mandela; the bloody riots in Sharpeville and Soweto; Biko's death; Mandela's release from jail; the all-race elections in 1994; and the rocky transition for the African National Congress from revolutionaries to parliamentarians with the levers of power in their hands.

Filed under generic topics, under place names, under personal names, political parties; row after row of cabinets pregnant with history. It's a task fast becoming a thing of the past; around the world digital technology is storing a newspaper's daily view on life without the fuss. The glue pots are being capped; the scissors and cutting blades collect dust in the storeroom. Now it's just the sound of disk drives whirring.

The *Argus*'s library was a labyrinthine place. Carter wandered over to the biographical section and pulled out the H drawer. He found an aged yellow folder of just half a dozen pages bearing the title 'Holmes à Court, Simon'. He leafed through it, instantly captivated by the mystery. There were a few stories of the trouble Simon had on the *Carina* in 1967 when he was lost at sea, and then of the search for Simon in 1977. Then the trail went cold, like a story half-told.

It seemed odd the story of what became of Simon had gone unwritten particularly in the Australian press, Carter thought; that we journalists who had so extensively covered the Holmes à Courts through the eighties and the nineties had never uncovered this story. Over the next few months Carter pieced together as much as he could about the mystery, following up contacts passed on by Roberton. He became a familiar sight at the *Argus* carrying around an old dog-eared folder of newspaper clippings and wandering into libraries, titles offices and maritime museums in an attempt to find something, anything he could, about the name Holmes à Court. He was trying to sniff out a lead, happy to have found a muse.

Carter had been a young journalist fresh out of cadet school when he attended Robert Holmes à Court's memorial service in the University of Western Australia's Winthrop Hall in 1990. Robert, aged fifty-three, had died in bed of a massive heart attack while at the Keysbrook stud on 2 September that year. Some say the pressure of trying to resurrect the family fortunes after the 1987 stockmarket crash led to his premature death, to say nothing of his smoking and diabetes. A sombre cast from Australia's *Who's Who* wandered into the beautiful building under the watchful gaze of the gryphons—mythical creatures that adorn the terracotta friezes around the outside of the hall, under the eaves. With the body and head of a lion and the wings of an eagle, they are said to be guardians. That September in brilliant sunshine, the medieval Romanesque arches and columns of Winthrop Hall glowed pastel hues. There were the pinks and creams of the sandstone and limestone, topped by the red clay-tile roof; vibrant scenes save for the silence and mourning of all those in black.

More than a thousand people attended the service. Carter kept his distance, sitting in the designated area for journalists inside the hall, and duly reported the towering eulogies to a man who to Perth seemed close to royalty. The hall was drowning in flowers. The diminutive Ethnée, now seventy-four, was there. She had tragically outlived both her sons. Carter's copy for Australian Associated Press was run in a number of newspapers, including the *Adelaide Advertiser* on 6 September 1990:

The very private life of Michael Robert Hamilton Holmes à Court has been glimpsed by the public in his death. His widow, Janet, was a stoic figure yesterday as she entered Winthrop Hall for her husband's memorial service.

Grief shaded by dark glasses, she leant on the arm of eldest son Peter, who will also be her aide in running the family's Heytesbury Holdings group.

Heytesbury Holdings general-manager Jon Elbury gave a rare and moving insight into the Holmes à Court enigma in his address. This publicly aloof and cold colossus of the business world was to friends and colleagues warm, loyal and compassionate and, above all, he had a wicked sense of humour.

Mourners learnt that Mr Holmes à Court, WA's richest businessman, never carried money in his pockets. A man of towering intellect, he was so fazed by today's technology that he once tried to turn up the TV volume with a calculator.

To illustrate the humour of the man called 'the boss', Mr Elbury told the story of a new employee who complained that demands of work meant there was not enough time to sleep. The boss replied: 'That's easily fixed—sleep faster.'

Carter was just twenty-three and had never met the man but passed him once in a corridor in 1988 when, as a media baron and owner of *The West Australian*, he came to see one of his editors, Tim Treadgold. He loped past, oozing confidence and wealth. They were heady days in Perth and to a cub reporter it was hard not to have starry eyes. Perth in the 1980s appeared to be at the centre of the world. In 1983 Alan Bond won the world's premier sailing tournament, the America's Cup, the first foreigner to do so, and four years later the world came to Fremantle, or at least it seemed that way, to win it back. Bond's money—shareholders' money, as it turned out—was being splashed about liberally. Then Bond lost the America's Cup defence, the stockmarket crashed in October 1987 and empires fell, including that of the Holmes à Courts.

There were acres of newsprint laid out in Australia for these men from Perth, interpreting and reinterpreting their lives and chasing the money trails. While the history of Robert Holmes à Court was written in the thousands upon thousands of column inches, the mystery at the heart of this family went unreported.

Carter figured the only thing to do was travel to Maun and try to track down the main characters, like Liversedge. The story was going nowhere in Cape Town. He sorted out his affairs, bade farewell to friends at the *Argus* and jumped on a train to Harare. It was May 1996 and the start of an African safari that would culminate in his arrival in Maun. Carter took the opportunity to see Africa—a 10 000-kilometre round journey, retracing some of the ground which Simon once travelled. The travel proved to be arduous but the majesty of Africa was revealed. From the huge volcanic crater in Tanzania which harbours so much of Africa's wildlife within its steep walls, to the magnificent mountain gorillas in the deep Ugandan jungle, this had been Simon's backyard.

Carter was expecting the final leg of the journey to Maun from Victoria Falls on the western corner of Zimbabwe to be tough, having been warned it could take days hitchhiking because of the lack of traffic. But fate lent a hand. He stood at a hitching post in Victoria Falls on a crisp early morning in late August and within minutes a truck driver pulled over and offered him a lift. The driver was heading to Johannesburg, about 1300 kilometres to the south. The route passed through the small junction town of Nata, the turning point for Maun. There Carter bade farewell to the truckie and within minutes was offered a ride by a bookseller from Gaborone.

By 5 pm that day Carter was in Maun pitching a tent on the rock hard ground in the precinct of the Sedia Hotel, a large cinder block establishment perched close to the wide and dry riverbed of the Thamakalane. It had been nearly four months since he'd left Cape Town. Maun was parched that August. The riverbed running through the centre of town was criss-crossed by four-wheel drive tracks. There was just one small watering well, with some local Batawana dropping buckets on ropes to get water. The droughts through the nineties in Maun had been extremely harsh. In the 1970s the river had been full—people could fish all year around.

Compared with the lush temperate zones to the north, Maun hardly felt like it was on the fringe of a wetland paradise, Carter thought. That night he ate at the hotel, took his notebook and spoke to some locals, asking who the town legends were and where he could find them. And Liversedge? They told Carter he still lived just down the river, with his wife June. Carter would set about tackling them all over the next few days.

He lay down in his tent on a bed of calcrete, upon which Maun sits, and tried to sleep. He was surrounded by village dogs, low-life mutts drooling and growling an arm's length away through the nylon. When they had quietened down and Carter was drifting off, one of the four-legged damnations ran headlong into the side of the tent, pulling out the pegs and landing on top of him. Through the nylon he frantically punched the thing off. He scrambled out and the pathetic dog stood yards away, stunned, its tongue lolling out of its mouth.

After reassembling the tent, he eventually slipped off to sleep but just before dawn a strange roar away in the distance awakened him. It was barely discernible at first but it was headed his way, down the riverbed and into town. For more than thirty minutes there was no other noise but what sounded like a distant wave rolling down between the banks where the Thamakalane should flow. In the darkness he tried to make sense of it. It was louder by degrees before it hit with a rush. A strong wind swept over him, buffeting his tent and straining the guy ropes before a few pegs sprang loose again. It faded for a moment and then hit again.

Carter fumbled for his torch to make a dash for the shelter of the nearby hotel, but within thirty seconds it had passed. He looked around, seeing nothing but the static shapes of African scrub and sensing nothing but the peace and cool air of the pre-dawn. The dogs had gone and the horizon was starting to glow; the sky was star speckled but its inky black was just starting to shift to blue. It was like nothing had happened. The African spirits were whispering. They were trying to tell him something.

A Town's Silence

August 1995

Shall man into the mystery of breath
From his quick beating pulse a pathway spy?
Or learn the secret of the shrouded death,
By lifting the lid of a white eye?
Cleave thou thy way with fathering desire
Of fire to reach to fire

Hymn to Colour, George Meredith

Town legend and hunter Lionel Palmer knew Simon well.
Carter had arrived on his doorstep and he agreed to chat,
despite a deep mistrust of writers. He felt he had been burned
by wildlife activists Mark and Delia Owens in their book *Cry
of the Kalahari*, which went into some detail about the drinking
in Maun in the seventies and described Lionel as something of
the cheerleader for the culture of the town.

They wrote: 'Lionel held considerable social position in
Maun. He was famous for his parties, where bedroom furniture sometimes ended up on the roof, and for his capacity for

scotch. Once after several days of intoxication, he woke up with a stabbing earache. The doctor at the clinic removed a 2-inch-long sausage fly—a reddish brown, tubelike, winged insect—which had taken up residence in Lionel's numbed ear while he slept off his drunkenness in a flowerbed.'

Palmer was a veteran who had managed to cope with the town's unique stresses and for Carter appeared willing to turn the other cheek—anything, it seemed, to have the opportunity to talk endlessly about the good old days in the Delta again. Palmer, in his late sixties, had been living in Maun for about forty years. He and his wife Phyliss held the record in Maun for being married the longest. There were fifty or so whites in Maun back in the fifties when Lionel arrived. He was originally a live-stock officer with the veterinary department and started hunting at weekends. In 1962 he started a hunting company called Safari South and was one of the great white hunters Wilbur Smith characterised. His company chaperoned wealthy clients from around the world, including the likes of Kerry Packer.

Lionel told Carter dozens of anecdotes about safaris, most of them humorous, like the time he was bringing a hunting client back to camp one evening. He was having trouble keeping the vehicle in a straight line and the impatient client asked, 'Why don't you let me have the steering wheel?' At that point Lionel did—literally. The steering wheel had shaken loose from its mounting as he bounced over the desert floor and he had been turning the wheels with brute strength using the friction of the steering column inside the shaft. The client hastily handed the steering wheel back to Lionel, who had kept his foot on the accelerator pedal the entire time.

And the legend of Lionel included the time when he had

a perfect score on safari of thirteen lions killed with thirteen bullets. The fourteenth shot he missed, wounding a lioness. 'I ran up a low anthill to see where she was and suddenly she charged: about a hundred yards in four seconds and there was no room for error.' Lionel dropped to one knee, positioned himself and sighted the lion. 'Once she was airborne I shot her and she landed behind me, dead.'

These days hunting is not a boast like it used to be. The court of public opinion has swung behind the conservationists. The town was divided, Lionel said, between the hunters on one side and the conservationists and filmmakers on the other. (In fact lion numbers fell so dramatically that the Botswana government put a ban on lion hunting in 2001 and powerful trophy hunters don't like that one bit—like George Bush Snr and Norman Schwarzkopf, who wrote to the government urging it to lift the ban.)

The hunting days and decades of hard living had caught up with Lionel. He was not exactly a handsome, craggy, ageing hero. When he greeted Carter at his house, nestled among a grove of trees on the banks of the Thamakalane River, he was wearing elastic stretch fabric on his legs after a big operation in the US to try to correct circulation problems. The surgeon was a client he had taken on safari.

Lionel, overweight and sporting a bulbous nose, showed Carter the outdoor bar, overlooking an expansive back lawn rolling down to the dry riverbed. It was the starting point, he said, of many a big night. There against the bar the beer, the bravado and the guns would be stacked high. Simon, however, was not part of the beer drinking set. He kept to himself.

'He was a very good friend of all of us,' Lionel said.

'He was a liked guy and did his job very well.' As a hunter, Lionel was a man Simon monitored. Game wardens like Simon would sometimes rub the hunters up the wrong way—he would have to take these hard-drinking, gun-toting men on if they and their clients were shooting animals outside hunting concession areas.

Simon was adept at making surprise raids on the hunting camps. 'If he had any kind of idea there was poaching or the law was being broken he would park his car miles away and walk through the swamps.' Simon would do this without a gun in areas full of lions and the extremely dangerous buffalo, just to catch the hunters unaware. 'You never had any idea when he would walk in—and in some of the most remote places,' Lionel said.

Carter asked if he had done that once too often. Was there a hunter with too much to lose? An angry shooter who lost his cool with Simon, someone Simon had made an enemy of? 'He was very thorough in his approach to his job. He was very strict but he was fair,' Lionel said. 'He wasn't the sort of guy that would victimise a certain group or company, not like a lot of game wardens. No, he was liked. He would sometimes socialise with us, but he was pretty much a loner.'

He told Carter that Maun had its share of intrigue. 'Wherever you have small communities there's always funny shenanigans going on. There are lots of divorces and what have you. All I can say about Maun is that if you ever lose your sense of humour you better quit. People say to me you always laugh about everything—well, there's nothing you can do sometimes but laugh. It can be mad here sometimes but you have got to roll with the punches and look at the lighter side of things.'

Then, when Carter started asking Lionel what he reckoned happened to Simon, Lionel grew hesitant. 'We thought maybe he had an accident in the bush.' When pressed about who knew what in Maun concerning Simon's activities, the shutters came down: 'I'm not mentioning any names. You know, you should remember it's best to let sleeping dogs lie.'

Later Bernie Truter arrived at Lionel's house. He was not in good shape. He had just been released from hospital and was recovering from horrific injuries to his legs after a terrible aircraft accident. He and son Grant had miraculously survived when their ultralight plane plunged to the ground, but it left them both with shattered legs. Carter asked Truter about Simon Holmes à Court. He just shrugged and hobbled away. He didn't want to talk about it.

Carter left Palmer's house that morning with the distinct feeling that Maun was going to be an exercise in bashing his head against a brick wall. He walked out onto the main road. There was one tarred road in Maun leading in and out of the town, and it hummed with the knobbly tyres of the speeding four-wheel drives of tourists, hunters and safari guides. They were often forced to slow down and veer around goats, the village dogs and donkeys—and there were plenty of donkeys in Maun. The least recalcitrant usually found themselves pulling rudimentary ploughs across the flood plain for the Batawana, who grew subsistence crops such as maize.

On each side of the tarred Matlapaneng Road, which in Simon's time was just a dusty track, battered beer cans glinted in the sunlight. Carter could see drink-driving was second nature among Maunites and the cans were obviously tossed from the window as they sped along. They were reused, though. Carter noticed that beer cans were used to reinforce mud walls on new rondavels. The huge number of cans being used around the villages was proof enough of the excessive drinking in the town. Carter was struck by the irony of these booze bricks—the detritus of a particularly Western problem breaking up so many homes had become a unique African solution in building them.

Carter made it into town. It was dusty and dominated by low-rise cinder block buildings. He found Riley's Garage— he had been told the night before all about the famous petrol station-cum-pub and trading post in town. Riley's was the first pub in northern Botswana. Ronnie Kayes, the owner of the garage, was there. His father Tom had lived in Maun for over sixty years. Tom's exploits included droving some 1000 head of cattle to Angola, a feat that took about seven months. He helped build the roads and houses in the district as long ago as the 1920s. The Kayes are even honorary members of the Batawana tribe. Ronnie, in his sixties, still ran the petrol station day-to-day and Carter found him there pushing paperwork in his office. 'Yes, I knew Simon, not that well, but he used to try to catch me when I was poaching,' said Kayes. 'He was very keen on one of the Wilmot girls,' he said. 'Daphne Wilmot. The Wilmots are a big name in town.' Tell me more, said Carter, but Kayes knew, or could remember, little else.

Carter sensed the veil coming down. The attitude of Palmer and Truter appeared to be setting a depressing standard. Over the next week Carter asked anyone who looked over fifty if they knew anything about Simon. Few people did, and they provided glib answers. Against intruders like Carter, the small town would draw its protective apron. Carter was particularly struck by Truter, why had he been so unwilling to talk, he wondered.

Of course there was one prominent name in the old newspaper clippings that Carter had to see: Tim Liversedge. He had found his telephone number in the Botswana phone directory and called. Carter was taken by surprise when Liversedge appeared happy to hear from him. 'There's an awful lot to be told about our exploits trying to trace him and there are many possibilities. It's an incredible mystery,' Liversedge said, as if already primed for the story. He explained to Carter he had long suspected that one day someone would come along asking questions.

Over the years Liversedge had achieved the success and fame in film that Simon once dreamt of when he sailed around the world in the *Maggie May*. He had taken Simon's lead and built a career on wildlife film documentaries. If Liversedge was not in Maun he could be found in a Hollywood studio or in Bristol, in the UK, the centre of wildlife film production there. He had built a long list of credits for the likes of National Geographic and the British Broadcasting Corporation, bringing his knowledge of the Okavango Delta and its incredible wildlife to a world audience. He had also become one of the world's leading experts on the Pels fishing owl—a rare sight in the Delta. Liversedge would be the first person to catch its incredible nocturnal fishing on film.

Carter ended up spending a lot of time with Liversedge. They first met at Maun airport, Liversedge offering to fly Carter to his film camp in the middle of the Delta. The handsome chaperone to Ethnée in the newspaper photos now had a beard and was thinning out on top. It was almost twenty years since those tumultuous events but as Carter was to discover, time had not dulled Liversedge's memory of Simon's disappearance.

Liversedge's Cessna sped down the runway, puncturing eddies of shimmering hot air swirling above the tarmac. He and Carter were on their way to his film camp in the heart of the Delta at Nxabega, about ninety kilometres north-west of Maun. The blinding heat in Maun that August gave no joy to anything—the Cessna's engine seemed to be sucking air furiously just to get them airborne.

After a buffeting, Liversedge levelled out, and within minutes he and Carter were high above the parched surrounds of Maun and then flying over the shimmering swamps of the great Okavango. Just a few hundred metres below, animals congregated around sporadically placed glistening pools, each watering hole boasting an awesome array of life and habitat. Elephants lay in mud baths; giraffes, their long necks looking like the third leg of an awkward tripod, would stoop to take a drink; and antelopes like the red lechwe stood among reeds in the marshes, while in other pools massive crocodiles lazed on the banks.

Each of these species was dotted along a vast plain interspersed with stately palms and oases of grass. Elsewhere, the landscape gave way to open dry earth defined by intersecting dotted lines. It is called the spoor, the animals' own highways and byways leading to the next watering hole: a landscape that looked every bit the inspiration for the indigenous circle and dot paintings of Aboriginal art in Australia.

'It's the driest I've seen in thirty years,' Liversedge said over the rhythmic drone of the engine. As if to underscore the point, a new vista opened up where the soil was a lifeless grey adjacent to stagnant patches of black water. But soon there were lush grasses and meandering tributaries again. As they flew on, it was like watching an African slide show, a world of flora and fauna and changing habitats wheeling and flickering below them.

Liversedge had been buzzing around Africa like this for decades. The aeroplane is now a standard form of transport for Maunites, many of whom make a living in the Delta either serving tourists or making films. Small, single-engined planes fly in and out of Maun all day long. The airport becomes as commonplace as a car park for suburban shoppers. A procession of gear is loaded and unloaded from planes as tourists and filmmakers go about their business. Flying becomes as natural as driving a car. Four-wheel drives make their way around the Delta too but the plane is the fastest way to get in—and the myriad of channels and tributaries make the Delta a dangerous place to drive when the floods start; in the dry it becomes a long, hard and hot slog through dusty, sandy terrain.

They had been heading due north from Maun for about thirty minutes—meandering occasionally when Liversedge would suddenly swoop low to the left or right if something of interest caught his eye—before Liversedge started to guide the plane down, bumping through thermals. Carter spied a dense thicket of bush below and a vehicle. The landing strip was nothing much more than a dusty track, but without fuss Liversedge brought the aircraft down. Liversedge's staff at the camp were there to meet them in an open-top Landrover.

Liversedge employed up to half a dozen people in the middle of the Delta, mostly to help protect the equipment stored there. There were several large fixed tents, one of which housed a massive IMAX camera for a forthcoming film. Liversedge was to mount this 60-kilogram beast onto a similarly impressive tripod fixed to his flat-bottomed air boat.

Liversedge and Carter settled in for the evening surrounded by the sounds of Africa, and over a bottle of cabernet sauvignon the story tipped out: Simon's life in the Delta; his sailing adventure around the world; his affair with Daphne and the unfounded suspicion that fell on Bernie Truter. 'No wonder Truter didn't want to speak with me,' Carter said. Then there was Simon's life as a Cold War spy, something that Liversedge had discovered after Simon's disappearance and which lent weight to the conspiracy theories about Simon's death. But there was something else that Liversedge told Carter that brought into stark relief the tragedy of Simon's disappearance.

Carter didn't sleep well that night. It wasn't just the noise of a riotous food chain at work outside his tent but the dangerous and disconcerting shapes one could just make out in the African night. They were shapes that by the morning's light turned out to be simply a fallen tree; the mad eyes of some wild beast just the glint from an old tin can discarded in the camp.

In the dead of night a predatory conspiracy filled the void. But the truth is usually much simpler than things the imagination invents.

Carter left Africa in 1996 empty handed. He didn't follow through. There were other places to go: a friend's wedding in Lake Tahoe, surfing in Mexico, scuba diving in Fiji. He kept travelling but often that night in the African bush would keep coming back to him. He could not shake it. It was as though the ghost of Simon Holmes à Court was on his back. It was years later, in January 2000, that he decided he would finally try to put the matter to rest.

The Forest's Tragic Secret

January 2000

Like one, on that lonesome road
Doth walk in fear and dread,
And having once turned around walks on,
And turns no more his head;
Because he knows, a frightful fiend
Doth close behind him tread
The Rime of the Ancient Mariner, Samuel Taylor Coleridge

The Boeing 737 descended into Port Elizabeth, bucking on a fierce headwind and then crabbed its way towards the runway at a crazy angle before it slammed onto the tarmac.

Carter picked up a hire car and headed towards the forest where so many secrets were hidden. The countryside on the drive down the N2 highway was uncannily similiar to Australia, like this was every bit the parallel universe, Carter thought; sharing a geographical history and two to three hundred years of frenetic colonial development, and an obvious legacy was the thing Carter was speeding along—

thousands upon thousands of kilometres of snaking black bitumen, vast stretches of road opening both countries up, tangled trails connecting the ports to the quarries.

This had been the last road for Steve Biko, and the last road for Simon Holmes à Court too.

The N2 highway sweeps out of Port Elizabeth, and within twenty kilometres the landscape starts to lift as great silent hills roll out in the distance. It was summer and the countryside was sparkling and verdant. The land had long since been cleared of indigenous trees, but pines and Australian eucalyptus trees had taken root, and the eucalypts jerked violently in the summer sou-wester: the signs on the long bridges that ford deep gorges warned motorists of strong crosswinds.

About forty-five kilometres out of Port Elizabeth Carter crested a hill and below a breathtaking world of ocean opened out to the left and a green floodplain to the right. The famous Jeffrey's Bay, one of the world's best surfing locations, stretched out before him. He sped along the N2, down the hill and onto the valley floor, and took the turn into the bay, heading to the surf break and breathing in the scene of the roaring Indian Ocean ahead. Carter grew up surfing and had surfed at Jeffrey's Bay in October 1995, arriving the day before a mighty double low-pressure system swooped along the coast. That was before he knew anything of the search he was to embark upon. To think I would be back here under these circumstances, trying to find a lost soul, Carter thought.

In 1995 he had thumbed a lift on the back of a farmer's pick-up from the highway and the driver, an ageing Afrikaner with a floppy straw hat who did not speak a word of English, dropped him off at the hostel in the centre of town. The hostel manager, a homely woman with a beaming smile, greeted him and said, 'They are expecting monster waves tomorrow,' as the needle barometer swept lower like a second hand in reverse. For two weeks Carter glided across the most perfect blue-green walls.

Now, it was the wrong end of the season. He could see that as he wound his way into town. A gale was racing across the ocean on a hot cloud-free day. The parallel to his home was unmistakeable: it was those heaving summer winds. He parked and had to push the door open against the gale, standing in the car park over looking the point. A wooden deck served as a viewing platform, nestled among a grove of proteas.

About one hundred feet below was the water's edge and among the craggy rocks surfers picked their way through the surging water, waiting for a lull in the waves before diving in with their surfboards as the ocean retreated, and before it mounted another tireless assault on the coast. Now, five years after his first visit, a couple of souls seek out a wave, but it's blown-out, windy and choppy, the sea whipped creamy-green. It would be like this over the ocean divide, out there to the east, Carter thought. Thousands of miles away there was a huge coastline baking in a southern summer, where afternoon winds buffet coastal towns like this one. But his family would be sleeping now, the west coast of Australia would be in darkness.

There was clearly no point hanging around, indulging in memories. Carter wanted to get to the Tsitsikamma before sunset. Back in his rent-a-car, he meandered out of J'Bay, past the holiday homes and the manicured lawns of this popular seaside resort, and before long was again cruising on the N2. It was an expansive landscape and a lonely one.

The broken white line swept under the car. Fate had driven him here and it felt impossible to stop. The Tsitsikamma ranges started to unfold. The mountains rose dramatically to the right of the road before the land plunged down towards the coast, the N2 bisecting the scene. This was just as Simon had seen it.

By late afternoon he arrived at a B&B at the village of Storm's River, still the quiet hamlet just off the main highway. Carter was only a few kilometres from the ocean and about twenty kilometres from the forest where Simon Holmes à Court's car was found.

Carter rented a log cabin and from his front porch the foothills of the Tsitsikamma rose hundreds of metres in front of him. It was a perfectly clear and still night. Through the trees behind him, a full moon ascended. It was so bright that soon everything looked to be cast in phosphorescence, throwing off a soft shadow.

Carter headed to the local inn and ordered fish and chips and a beer, and couldn't help but overhear the conversations at tables nearby, including one occupied by two middle-aged, sunburnt English couples. An entire conversation between the four people, which to his ear rumbled along as a monologue in a north England accent: 'Has it got aircon? If it hasn't got aircon there's no point considering it. We have to have aircon. Oh I think you should have aircon. At that price, it must, surely. Oh yes, I should think so. I think I should phone and check. Yes, maybe you should. Must have aircon. I mean at that price. Yes, God, remember Turkey? A million lira was £1.20. Ridiculous really. Stupid currency. What were the hotels like? Aircon? Brilliant really, they do that well.'

Package tourists like this flock to the Tsitsikamma, an area protected from the rampant forestry industry. Despite some measures in recent years to control what had been an utterly reckless destruction of the area, all the way down the highway Carter passed kilometres of pine plantations where once massive yellow-wood trees grew.

Carter was in bed relatively early, after a day of travelling, and slept well until he woke in a cold sweat at about 5 am. Was it the African spirits whispering again? He had a nightmare so disturbing that he wondered what awaited him in the forest. He dreamt a large black dog was in his room and had started running towards him. In a dreamscape where time is bent and distance is irrelevant, the rabid dog's lunge towards him from just across the room seemed to take minutes. Carter woke before it reached him but he was frozen with fright, lying rigid, wondering what demons lurked.

He was not usually prone to this sort of paranoia and was determined to shrug off his own fears. He dressed and walked outside and watched the sun rise as a red-eyed dove perched on an electrical wire above him, singing coo-coo, ka coo-coo-coo, repeating it tirelessly as the sun filtered through the trees. The tune, which ornithologists equate to 'I-am, a red-eyed-dove', had been a constant companion to Carter in Africa in the years before and he took comfort from it.

Deciding to take a stroll, Carter walked out from the B&B and crossed the N2 highway to the foothills of the Tsitsikamma. The area was a national park, one of the few protected from logging. The sunrise was catching the tops of the hills and the shadows started to run from the valleys. The air was cool and Carter's breath misted.

The huge straight trunks of yellow-wood and stinkwood trees shot high above a thick forest alive with the chatter and tunes of not only doves but hundreds of other companions: thrushes, orioles, Cape wagtails, pipits, cuckoos and the magnificient Knysna lourie, with its emerald green and crimson plumage.

For hours Carter explored tracks in this patch of sun-dappled Eden. Beads of morning dew adorned every stem, leaf, twig and flower, forming strings of diamonds on spiders' webs. In this temperate zone mosses soften the jagged remains of fallen trees and extraordinary fungi, like satellite dishes, bloom from the forest floor. Then there was the tourist attraction of the not so imaginatively named Big Tree, an 800-year-old yellow-wood, nearly 40 metres tall with a nine-metre girth.

Standing in that natural wonder it was easy to forget time but at around 9 am, having seen no one else, Carter's reverie was suddenly broken by the rumble of a timber truck. He emerged from the forest and found that after a few hours of scouting around he had made his way back towards the N2. He walked down the highway to pick up the car.

About twenty kilometres west down the N2, past the enormous sheds of the Boskor sawmill and a wasteland thanks again to recent clearing, there was a road to the right, the R102 to Coldstream. A few kilometres on, Carter spied a sign to the Lottering Forestry Station. According to the tired old press clippings he carried around, Carter knew he was near the picnic spot where Simon Holmes à Court's car had been found.

Down a rough gravel road and on the fringe of a huge pine plantation sat a lone cream-coloured cement-brick building—

the office of the forestry managers for the district. It was still fairly early, around 10 am, but the sun was high and already it was a baking hot day. Carter made his way into the building. It was cool inside and he could hear conversations in Afrikaans filtering down the central hallway. Off the small entrance lobby was a large room with a wooden inquiry counter. Fans turned slowly and the walls were adorned with foresty maps. 'Hello, can I help you?' said a man sitting at a desk with a two-way radio. Dressed in khaki shorts and shirt, the man walked over, hand outstretched, and introduced himself as Henry.

Carter explained that he was a journalist investigating the disappearance of a man in the area twenty years earlier. Henry was intrigued and without fuss, or indeed without the suspicious eye that Carter had received in Maun, Henry jumped onto the two-way radio again, contacting rangers in their 4WDs to see if anyone remembered much about it. Henry told Carter to come back in the afternoon to see what they had come up with.

He drove to where Storm's River meets the ocean. It was ten degrees cooler there—a thick marine fog blanketed the area but Carter could make out the dramatic cliffs and the indigenous forests rising high above the ocean. Here the dark rivers of the Tsitsikamma ran through magnificent gorges, to meet a restless Indian Ocean. Carter waited out much of the day on a rocky outcrop, watching black oyster catchers pecking their way around him, and a Cape claw otter playing in the ocean.

By mid-afternoon Carter was back at Lottering, crunching up the gravel road and wondering if there would be any news for him. Would it be a dead end? What were the chances that anyone was still working here from that time, twenty years ago?

Another forestry worker, a supervisor, Barry, was waiting for Carter. 'Hello, you're the chap who wanted to know about the man who disappeared? We found someone, she works on a nearby farm, her manager is driving her over here.' Barry was reviewing the press cuttings. 'Who was this guy? What did he do?' He told Carter the Tsitsikamma forest was a place in which someone could easily disappear—there had been other disappearances over the years.

It was then that Lorenda Savage walked in, looking nervous and speaking only Afrikaans. Lorenda had responded when one of her bosses asked if anyone knew about the case of a man disappearing near the Vark River twenty years earlier. The community grapevine had worked fast.

Lorenda was a labourer on a nearby farm and lived in one of the timber workers' cottages in a village set aside for about 400 employees. They were all defined by their mixed race—'coloureds'. It's a small township rife with alcohol abuse and domestic violence. After a generation of discrimination these people had been given little hope for anything other than a life of performing menial chores for low wages. Lorenda bore the scars—she had bad burns on her left arm and her tired eyes reflected a life of hard work, no luxury and a terrible home life. Barry spoke of vicious arguments in the workers' village and the boiling water burns inflicted by drunken men and women on one another.

Lorenda, wearing a yellow tee-shirt and blue workers' pants, had just finished a shift, working in the fields. Carter began asking her questions and Barry interpreted for him.

Carter immediately had to set about allaying Lorenda's fears, telling her he was not associated with the police. That Lorenda had an innate distrust of the forces was hardly surprising given the history of South Africa.

Carter showed Lorenda a photograph from a newspaper clipping depicting Simon's car and immediately her face twisted up and she turned away. To Carter the reaction indicated that this woman had a deep connection to the story; it had awakened some bad memories. She explained to Carter what had happened that day when she was still only seventeen years old—the trip to the forest to look for brush only to discover a skeleton. Of the people there that day, Lorenda was the only one left alive to tell the story. Her friends had gone—Bernadine was murdered in the Eastern Cape and Beryl had been struck down by a mysterious illness. Of the two men who had been eel fishing and rushed to the girls' aid, Jim Swaart had died in a bushfire and Jaap Fick too had passed away. The forestry manager, Pierre Theron, died when, standing by a logging truck one day, the load broke and he was crushed. Carter thought it was as if they had all been cursed.

Carter asked Lorenda to take him to the site and, with Barry, they drove to the area. Back on the R102 they passed the picnic spot just beyond which Simon's car had been found in 1977, and then made their descent, a winding road that took them to a valley floor and a small bridge. Carter checked the odometer—three kilometres exactly from the picnic spot. Lorenda told Carter to turn into a small track near the bridge and they parked the car.

It was cool and quiet under a magnificent canopy of trees. They made their way down a harvesting track, struggling through thick ferns and creepers for about ten minutes, walking upriver and away from the bridge. With little hesitation Lorenda stopped and pointed to an area near the base of a huge yellow-wood tree. *'Dit was daar iewers*—it was somewhere here,' she said. Carter asked her the position of the skeleton and she said: 'Lying this way,' and she traced a line with her arms, indicating that Simon's feet were facing the Vark River bridge.

And there was one other thing next to the skeleton, Lorenda said: a gun—a shotgun was found with Simon's body that day in February 1980 . . .

Lorenda, just seventeen and distraught, huddled with her friends as the police arrived to inspect the remains. They cleared the bracken and noted the position of the gun. It was lying across the bones of the left hand. It was a shotgun with one cartridge spent. They inspected the weapon: a Webley & Scott 410 shotgun.

The top of the skull was missing. It looked like suicide but the police couldn't rule anything out—it could have been a murder made to look like suicide.

From where Simon had fallen there was a perfect view of the bridge across the Vark River—the police didn't appreciate the significance but Bodo Muche would have. The image would haunt him, like some tragic testimony to his nightmare all those years before.

Major Eric Strydom, then head of the Port Elizabeth murder and robbery squad, surveyed the scene and remembered the case of the missing sculptor from Botswana. He was sure the skeleton was that of Simon Holmes à Court. Back at the station Strydom went through the file and called Liversedge with the shocking news, arranging to meet him in Johannesburg the following week. Liversedge was devastated. Simon was not the type of man to take his own life.

The police started conducting forensic tests on the weapon. Strydom had his team trace the registration on the gun. He had the results by the time he met Liversedge. They met at the Hillbrow police station in the centre of Johannesburg. There was a box of belongings and Liversedge recognised Simon's tattered clothing and his shoes. Strydom then asked Liversedge if he knew Daphne Truter? Yes, why? Strydom picked up the Webley & Scott 410. 'This is hers. It was found with the body.'

Liversedge had to sit down. He was furious. Daphne? In all this time Daphne had not reported her gun missing. How had Daphne forgotten about that? Strydom asked Liversedge if his friend had been depressed when he went missing.

'We are continuing our investigations although we are reasonably sure that Mr Holmes à Court committed suicide. The shotgun found next to the body had a discharged cartridge in one barrel and an unused cartridge in the other.'

The folk in Maun greeted this with disbelief. Liversedge had returned to Maun and the news spread quickly. He stormed over to Daphne's house demanding answers. She was weeping, she had only just heard from the police. Her legendary father Bobby Wilmot had given the gun to her—

she had no idea it was even missing, she wailed. Liversedge was dumbfounded. Daphne, sobbing, told Liversedge that Simon must have taken the gun when he left that morning while she was busy with breakfast and getting Grant ready for school. He had walked out of the house alone.

'I don't even remember him using it, ever. But he knew I had one. I used it to shoot snakes. It just never dawned on me it was missing.'

'For three years?' Liversedge asked, incredulous.

'Oh, Simon, what a terrible, terrible thing to do. I didn't believe for one minute that he could have been so unhappy to do something like this. We had a tremendous time together, maybe he really couldn't face not being a part of that anymore.

'It's just a shame we didn't actually talk about our relationship more before he went off. It wasn't like we weren't to have anything more to do with each other, it's just that it was coming to an end.

'You know, I remember going to a party and dancing quite a lot with another guy and Simon thought I was having more fun with someone else. Do you know, I don't even remember specifically what we were arguing about when he left that day. I don't remember him even putting up a fight about our relationship and saying, please, don't end it, or anything like that. But it was getting a bit out of hand and I wasn't divorced yet.'

Daphne was puzzled about why Simon had driven as far as he did. Simon must have wanted to cover his tracks and conceal the identity of his vehicle. Perhaps he did just want to die alone, she said. Liversedge shook his head and walked out.

The question of why she never reported her gun missing would nag him for the rest of his life.

No one in Maun wanted to believe Simon could have done such a thing. They all felt so guilty.

The police telephoned Ethnée. It was a call—like the one three years before—that any mother dreads. But the news of a weapon found next to Simon did not diminish her belief that Simon had been murdered. She said her son did not have suicidal tendencies. She would tell the South African press: 'I will never rest until I've found my son's murderer. If the skeleton is his, he was murdered, and I intend finding out who did it, and why. The news of the discovery was a tremendous shock and the circumstances of his disappearance worrying. All I know for sure is that he did not commit suicide.'

Within weeks forensic tests were conducted and from the remains experts ascertained the height and weight of the deceased. It was the only ID ever done. The measurements matched Simon's. Ethnée's cousin in South Africa, Dr Paul Oates, arranged for Simon's remains to be cremated and the ashes sent to Ethnée in Perth. She organised a ceremony, met up with Simon's old sailing friend Milton Skinner, and along with Ethnée's new partner, Ronnie Critchley—a lifelong friend from Africa who emigrated to Australia and married Ethnée in 1978, the year after Simon disappeared—they sailed in Skinner's boat into the Indian Ocean off the coast of Perth and scattered Simon's ashes. Robert did not want to go. Ethnée retained some of Simon's ashes and scattered them around a tree near one of the dams at Keysbrook, where Simon had once fished when he stayed at the property while working on his documentary.

To the police, suicide appeared more plausible than Simon being a victim of a Cold War conspiracy to eliminate him, or that his death came at the hands of some bandits in the region, notwithstanding the political and social strife around the time of Steve Biko's death.

But questions remained. One that his friends and his mother continually asked—why did he drive so far south? Why was there so much effort to conceal the identity of the vehicle? On the first point, the Challis theory—that he had headed south to live in Tony Challis's shack for a while—had some merit because, just maybe, this rugged individualist was simply heartbroken and the horrendous storm that whipped through the area as he arrived could hardly have lifted his spirits.

Some of Simon's friends were incredulous that Simon would have felt so hurt by Daphne's rejection. But why was there an attempt to remove the identification on the vehicle? Did Simon do that himself? If so, it displayed a steely premeditation of the final tragic end. It could never be fully explained, other than if it was suicide, as the police suspected, Simon went to extraordinary lengths to try to ensure no one found out.

The Tsitsikamma forest is a magical place on the southern tip of Africa marked only by its anonymity and as the keeper of secrets as to what befell an extraordinary character in a family so prominent in the public domain in Australian life. There was nothing to celebrate the area for its place in a tragic history. Just the whisper of the breeze and the call of the bird life amid haunting memories of a life that ended so brutally.

Carter could sense Lorenda was growing impatient to leave—there were, after all, unpleasant memories here for her. They drove back to her cottage and Carter thanked her for her time. She looked slightly bemused at the foreigner wanting to go over this old ground. It was obvious it would be a big topic among the workers in the village that night.

Carter dropped Barry back at the Lottering Forestry Station and he told Carter how Lorenda was clearly disappointed that not much had come of his visit. 'What do you mean?' Carter asked. He said there had been a reward offered for any information that led to the discovery of Simon Holmes à Court and it remained a sore point for her—grafting out a living as a labourer on the timber plantations and the farms in the area—that nothing had ever been forthcoming.

The sun was setting, blanketing the Tsitsikamma ranges in a saffron glow. Amid lengthening shadows and the silence of dusk, Carter decided to drive back to the area alone after bidding farewell to Barry. It took an effort to suppress a sense of foreboding about going back to Simon's resting place, and Carter's imagination was running into overdrive with dark thoughts about omens and curses.

He parked in the same spot they had just left a few hours earlier, and walked to where Lorenda had shown him the position of the skeleton. It was such a peaceful place for such a dramatically violent event. Carter sat looking at the bridge and was quickly overwhelmed by awful and tragic images of a man sitting in the same spot; a man who may have felt he had nothing left to live for. Could that really have been the way it ended? Carter sat there in emptiness. There was a void, impossible to quantify.

How was he to make some kind of peace with a place rent with human tragedy? Absentmindedly he fumbled through his wallet, brimming with foreign coins. Carter took three gold-coloured coins—Australian, English and Botswanan—and scattered the three into the bush where Simon had died. Maybe it was an empty gesture, but perhaps three talismans from three parts of the world represented some kind of reunification for a wandering soul. 'Rest in peace, Simon. Rest in peace,' he said.

The light was starting to escape the valley. Carter walked through reaching creepers and the grasp of ferns to get back to the car. He drove out overwhelmed by the events of the day and wondering if the search for the truth about Simon Holmes à Court had finally come to an end. The only conspiracy was the conspiracy of silence, out of a sense of respect and maybe guilt from those who had ever been close to him.

The next morning Carter wandered through the Storm's River village to the local police station, the sleepy constabulary where the investigation had begun all those years before. He met acting station commander, Henk de Vos, a towering man of two metres who, like many in the South African police force, was not only an Afrikaner but boasted an impressive moustache, seemingly de rigueur in local police forces. There were photos of rugby teams surrounding Inspector de Vos. The blotter-cum-calendar on his pine desk was two and a half years out of date.

Carter asked Inspector de Vos if there were any records at Storm's River about the case and after about ten minutes searching the files in a room full of cabinets he came up with nothing. He added that the docket, or case documents, on the death of someone was never closed if it was an unsolved murder. It would only be destroyed after ten years if an inquest found accidental death or suicide.

Carter headed to Port Elizabeth and the local library. Searching on microfiche he found old newspaper clips that he had missed until that point—explaining the discovery of Simon's skeleton. Reports that a gun had been found with Simon had been there all along.

Later Carter called Inspector de Vos's counterpart at Port Elizabeth, Inspector Erasmus. The inspector told Carter an inquest had been held and a 'J56' issued—the form used when the inquest is closed. 'The entry in the register was that no one else was responsible for the cause of death,' Inspector Erasmus said. What did that mean? It meant the police felt it was either suicide or an accident. Simon Holmes à Court's case was closed years ago, he said.

Daphne's Lament

This Hermit good lives in that wood
Which slopes down to the sea
How loudly his sweet voice he rears!
He loves to talk with marineres
That come from a far countree
The Rime of the Ancient Mariner, Samuel Taylor Coleridge

Carter had heard in Maun that Daphne was now living in Johannesburg. She had divorced Bernie in 1981 and was remarried to a pilot called Klaus Hildebrandt. He tracked down her phone number. She didn't seem that surprised to hear from him—news had travelled that someone was researching the mystery. They agreed to meet but Daphne had one condition—she was to clear it with Ethnée first.

Carter flew back to Johannesburg the next day, leaving the tragedy of Tsitsikamma behind him. He only had a few more days left in South Africa before returning home to Perth. He wanted to meet Ethnée there, to close the story.

He called Daphne. 'Ethnée feels it's okay for me to meet you.' Carter was looking forward to laying out the whole mystery in front of the woman who probably knew Simon best, certainly in the last few months of his life.

From the airport Carter headed to Brixton, a cosmopolitan and mixed race suburb just to the west of the city, dropping his bags with an acquaintance there, and caught another cab to Sandton. He had arranged to meet Daphne in a coffee shop in a plaza of the giant Sandton shopping centre. Daphne arrived wearing blue jeans and a blue and white checked shirt. She was a little over five foot, glamorous, with a soft smile and gentle eyes. She was confident and assured.

'Hello, Daphne, it's great to have the chance to finally talk,' Carter said.

Daphne nodded. 'How was Maun?' she asked, and they embarked on a preliminary course of small talk about his time in Africa and, as is common in a place so dominated by the elements, the weather.

'You can ask me anything you like; anything, I won't be offended,' Daphne finally said. Carter asked her about Simon's Cold War activities, his spying and the suspicions that it might have had something to do with his death.

'He mentioned he was doing some undercover work,' Daphne said. 'I didn't go into what he was doing. He vaguely mentioned it and it sounded so clandestine that I didn't want to go into it. I wanted nothing to do with that so I didn't press him any further.' Daphne said she had also heard rumours that rather than spy work Simon might have been involved in smuggling endangered species—it was the first time Carter had heard of that.

Daphne said she did not know her gun was missing all that time. 'It was only when they told me what make it was, when they found it, that I realised.'

She believed what few of Simon's friends and family wanted to—that Simon had taken his own life.

'You try to go back over in your mind what could have happened and why he felt like that to have done that, and when he could have gotten the gun because it was locked in the store all the time. And you think, when could that have happened and why?'

Daphne remained close to Ethnée over the years but said Ethnée could never accept the possibility that Simon had committed suicide. 'She would not believe it.' But then, what mother would?

Daphne's frank assessment of her falling out with Simon was a disturbing conclusion to a long search for an answer to the mystery of Simon Holmes à Court. She said Simon was very unhappy in relationships.

'I wasn't divorced at the time and the pressure from Bernie and pressure from Simon . . . well, after a while it was easier for me to cool it down. I think Simon hadn't had a lot of girl-friends. I do believe he loved me very dearly, although I guess I didn't believe it at the time.

'Bernie was threatening to come down and live in Maun— he was living in Shakawe. Then it was not right for me to be seen in this situation because Simon was living next door.

'No one really believed that he was not just on a walkabout. Then it became quite obvious that he was missing.'

Whereas some might still have worried about how they could have helped avoid a catastrophe, Daphne had come to terms with it all. Women like Daphne, growing up in Africa, are tough. She was not particularly used to dwelling on a past haunted by such tragedy and she struggled to define the emotion of those long-ago events. She had moved on. It was like she had an armour of Victorian-age resoluteness. Carter asked how she felt in her heart about Simon Holmes à Court.

'He was a super lovable, romantic, warm person. He had brilliant blue eyes, a lovely face, a rugged face. He was like the Camel cigarette man. He was softly spoken and a wonderful person. We had so many lovely moments.

'There are lot of ifs and maybes and if I had done this, maybe that would have changed or whatever. I feel if we had spoken about our relationship more. You know, there was nothing said, there was nothing really like: this is the end of us or anything like that, it wasn't a case of that at all. I just remember there being tremendous pressure, of me feeling the tremendous pressure of Bernie coming back to Maun, and with my relationship with Simon. I just wanted out. I just wanted out of the relationship.

'I guess I had no idea he had fallen so deeply. I think having had so few girlfriends and relationships in his life that this was probably something that meant a tremendous amount to him.'

Liversedge would forever remain bemused about why Daphne never accounted for a missing weapon. Daphne could never quite explain it. Liversedge maintained that—after the news that Simon's remains had been found with her shotgun in 1980—Daphne suddenly recalled Simon had asked her for the gun to shoot a boomslang, a common snake in Botswana.

Daphne never realised it had been missing for so long. She was going through a break-up, was moving house and was raising a son—perhaps events at the time overwhelmed her and she simply failed to report it, assuming that, like a lot of lost property, it would simply turn up. From a hunting family and growing up with guns, cavalier attitudes like this were of no real surprise.

But like Daphne, Liversedge had come to accept that Simon probably ended his own life. 'Simon was outwardly a rugged, very strong-willed person, but when it came to matters of the heart, he probably wasn't—he was something else.'

Carter flew back to Perth with a heavy heart. He found suicide hard to accept. There remained unanswered questions. Not everyone who chooses a desperate cry for help like suicide leaves a note, but would they go to such extraordinary lengths to never be found? The question kept burning.

Once in Perth he drove to the village of Keysbrook, about ninety minutes to the south-east, to meet Ethnée. She greeted him warmly.

They sat on the back patio of her sweet cottage, the original house on the estate, sheltered under the shade of the tall *eucalyptus grandis*—also known as rose gums—whose trunks glow with pastel hues. It was nearing sunset and a warm amber radiance, like in Africa, started to diffuse the hard white light of the day. Over tea they chatted about Carter's journey as the guinea fowl and a peacock wandered about her expansive backyard.

Ethnée described how Simon's case files were still open at the Hillbrow Police Station in Johannesburg, but Carter told her that was not what he had found—that the police at Port Elizabeth had said the case was closed. The statement hung there between them.

'And how did you find Daphne?' Ethnée asked.

Carter said she was a tough lady of Africa. Ethnée laughed.

'Yes, she's very tough. She knows the bush backwards. That's where she and Simon hit it off actually. She's not afraid of anything.'

Carter asked her what she knew about Simon's mental state prior to his disappearance.

'He was fine,' she said, saying Simon and Daphne were very much in love. She told Carter that Daphne had told her she felt the two might have got married if he was still alive.

'Simon wrote to me and said he was now living in a grass hut,' she says of the rondavel Simon was renting from Lloyd Wilmot, Daphne's brother. 'Simon's foundry was just about ready to operate. He was very happy and very settled there.'

Ethnée has maintained her interest in spirituality and has regular sessions with clairvoyants, often asking them about Simon. 'Every single clairvoyant I've been to says Simon did not commit suicide. Tim Liversedge was the only one who thought he did and Bodo Muche was convinced he did not.' She asked Carter what he thought. He said he couldn't say.

Despite the conclusion of the police, too many questions remained to be certain.

Tragedy has tracked Ethnée, with so many men close to her dying throughout her lifetime. She has outlived her two sons and lost the three men she loved most in her life: Peter Holmes à Court, Charles Trevor and Lieutenant Colonel Ronnie Critchley.

Ethnée remains active and involved in the horse stud at Heytesbury. She regularly visits the memorial to Robert on the property established by her daughter-in-law Janet. The memorial is marked by the words: 'I stood among them but not of them. In a shroud of thoughts which were not their thoughts.' The words could equally apply to his brother Simon.

Head due west from that point, crossing the Indian Ocean and following the sun, and landfall would be around Storm's River near the forest that holds the secret of Simon Holmes à Court. While Robert's memorial is a grand artistic affair, at the place where Simon disappeared in Africa there is nothing to define an extraordinary life, other than the beauty of the forest and an ancient yellow-wood tree that rises from the forest floor.

Who can say for sure what happened to Simon Holmes à Court that bleak night in 1977? But it was a lonely and tragic end to the life of an adventurer who died with a broken heart but in the bosom of the grand lady who knew him best: Mother Nature.

Epilogue:
An Old Friend Returns
2004

For those who are dreaming of similar adventures, there can only be one piece of advice—put your dreams into practice; the first step is always the hardest but the eventual rewards make it all well worthwhile.

Simon Holmes à Court

Liversedge and his wife June decided to head to Cape Town in early 2004 to take a break after completing a three-year film project *Roar: The Lions of the Kalahari*. They were about to embark on a world tour to promote the film and decided to spend a few days relaxing in Cape Town beforehand.

On a brilliant summer's day they headed out of town towards Boulders Beach, famous as the site of an African penguin colony located near the southern tip of the African continent. They stopped for lunch at a small restaurant overlooking the Indian Ocean in a historic navy port near Boulders Beach. Liversedge ordered a beer and surveyed the scene. He

picked up his birdwatching binoculars and was absentmindedly examining the yachts moored nearby in the protected bay.
Suddenly Liversedge leapt out of his chair.

'Bloody hell, June! It's the Maggie May.'

'What? It can't be, let me look,' said June.

It was a ketch, with the distinctive two masts and small
cabin. June rubbed her eyes in disbelief. Emblazoned on the
hull was 'Maggie May'.

Liversedge rushed out of the restaurant to the club.

The owner was English, one of the club members told him,
but he wasn't there. He had gone into the city.

Liversedge would eventually make contact with the owner,
who checked the logbooks. Data was missing about the old sea
dog's history, but Liversedge was convinced it was Simon's old
yacht.

Stranger still is that this bizarre coincidence should have
occurred in the famous old navy village named after the first
governor of the Cape: Simon's Town. Truth is always stranger
than fiction.

What Happened to Them?

Liversedge has made a success of his film career and is still based in Maun, as the conclusion of this narrative explained. Daphne settled in Johannesburg. Ethnée, now eighty-nine, still lives on the estate at Keysbrook, surrounded by photos of her sons, grandchildren and great-grandchildren. There are some of Simon's bronze sculptures on her coffee table and bookshelves too and of course plenty of photos of her other son Robert who had created such a successful corporate life in Australia.

Robert had decided from an early age that the independence movements sweeping Africa would not, in the end, favour a white man with entrepreneurial ideas and he decided to search for opportunity elsewhere. At just nineteen he left Africa bound for New Zealand, travelling via Australia by ship, managing to catch the 1956 Melbourne Olympic Games before arriving in Auckland, New Zealand, to study forestry. He did not see that through, however, and returned to South Africa after travelling to England, financed thanks to a legacy of an uncle of Ethnée's, available to him when he was twenty-one.

But after trying his hand at a restaurant business in Cape Town and studying law by correspondence from the hotel resort his mother had established with her new husband Charles Trevor, Robert quit Africa for Australia in 1962. He studied law in Perth and for a time was an undistinguished lawyer. But Robert was a charmer and his life in the society set established connections that would soon come in handy.

In 1970 he acquired the WA Woollen Mills in Albany, about a four-hour drive south of Perth. He persuaded the state government of the day to waive its rights as a secured creditor for $500 000 in return for keeping the mill running and employees' jobs safe. It was a fantastic deal. The mill's operations were restructured and it turned out to be a money-spinner—the first step for the man who became known in Australia's business community as the Great Acquirer. He then hit the business establishment's radar screen in 1974 when the mining boom in Australia collapsed and the civil engineering and transport company Bell Group found itself in trouble.

In a move that Robert would become famous for, he raided the company, unseating the family owners, and established a publicly listed vehicle that would serve him well over the next decade—Bell Group Ltd. With Bell Group and sister company Bell Resources, Robert carved out an empire that would go on to make some tilts at the world's largest companies.

It was the 1987 stockmarket crash that unseated Robert and he was estimated to have lost more than $1 billion in the precipitous plunge in share prices that October. But he had assets to realise, not least of which was his 30 per cent stake in mining giant BHP and an array of other international assets.

Some say it was the stress of the stock market crash, others his heavy smoking and lack of exercise. Both are surely true. In the early hours of 2 September on the Heytesbury ranch, Janet woke to a sudden roar of breath—it was Robert's last, at the age of fifty-three. Janet frantically called for an ambulance and a husband-and-wife team of country ambulance volunteers arrived soon after 4 am and tried desperately to revive Robert during the 20-kilometre drive to the Armadale-Kelmscott hospital. He was pronounced dead minutes after arriving at the hospital. He was survived by Janet, their four children and, of course, Ethnée.

Bodo Muche had emigrated to Australia in August 1978 after meeting and marrying Robyn, an Australian. Now, more than twenty-five years later, Muche stills finds he has to hold back the tears about Simon Holmes à Court's strange disappearance. Muche lives on a property north-west of Brisbane, in Queensland about two hours drive up the Bruce Highway from the capital. A gravel road leads to a house nestled on the side of a hill well away from the main road. Muche has a large workshed where he wiles away the hours sculpting. If you were to visit him there he would probably emerge from it and offer an earnest and solid handshake, and an easy smile. His sculptor's hands are strong and supple, except for his right thumb; it has a fleshy glove on it and no fingernail—a legacy of his trade. A blade on an angle grinder Muche was once using snapped and sliced right through his thumb, leaving it hanging only by skin.

Fortunately surgeons were able to save it. A sculptor needs his thumbs. A long scar runs up his inner forearm where the surgeons took some of his radiata bone to rebuild it.

Muche is a tough looking man, bearded and fit, with a youthful gait and bright eyes that belie his sixty-five years. Muche has built a business sculpting, among other things, big game fish like marlin and sailfish. He has secured the rights to big game fishing tournaments all over the world as trophy maker—large bronze works awarded to the tournament winners. It's a lucrative trade since tournaments like those hosted by Rolex are the province of the rich and famous, with million dollar boats—and million dollar entry fees. From his tin workshed, Muche is playing his part in this globalised world: his game fish are shipped out to adorn the mantelpieces of the rich and famous in mansions ranging from Europe to the US.

Muche's main competitor for this lucrative market for trophies and commissions is the other Maun veteran, Kent Ullberg, and the two, while old friends, are fiercely competitive when trying to win clients for their work. But Muche and Ullberg agree that if Simon was alive today, he too would have become a great sculptor.

As former taxidermists in Botswana, Muche and Ullberg know their animals. While Ullberg settled in Corpus Christie, Texas, Muche and his partner Robyn settled in an area that is known not so much for kangaroos and platypus that are common in the hills and its creeks below, but it's big deer population, introduced more than one hundred years ago. 'I have hunting access over thousands of acres here,' Muche says. He will stalk the red deer on foot, and usually alone. There appears to be symmetry in that. Muche has neatly closed the circle on his heritage, given that his forebears used to hunt deer around Dresden in Germany. Muche's modest house might be a world away from the gothic steeples and arches of central Europe, but it shares something with the homes of his ancestors—it bristles inside and out with deer antlers, not just as decoration but as towel racks and door handles too. 'Nothing is wasted,' Muche said.

Muche has a finely turned radar, a perceptive ability that one might call a sixth sense of the kind that drives animals crazy well before an earthquake strikes, or causes dogs to start barking before a storm hits. Muche's extraordinary dream about Simon still haunts him. It has left Muche with a feeling of helplessness that maybe he could have done something to save Simon from his fate. 'After the car was found Tim Liversedge and I went over and over it, again and again. We both thought he had been murdered,' Muche said.

What of the gun found with Simon? Muche is at a loss for words. Was the gun planted? he asked. He knew little of Simon's spying activity but reveals that in the mid-seventies Simon was thrown in jail in Francistown under suspicion of being a spy. Simon was released the next day and nothing came of it, but the Botswana authorities accused him of being either a South African or Rhodesian agent. Muche was the only person who Carter ever interviewed who knew of this event. Simon was released without being charged. As far as Muche knew, Simon was never bothered again.

One can only guess, but the root of this state-sanctioned intimidation could have lain with Simon's lack of commitment to the new Botswana. That's because in 1975, Simon had not long returned to the country after an extended period away thanks to his sailing adventure on the *Maggie May*. The Botswana authorities were probably suspicious of his activities while he was outside the country. It again raises more questions and adds more fuel to the fire for those close to Simon who believe there was a conspiracy to eliminate him. Muche and Liversedge remain friends, but on Simon's fate they disagree. Muche say he must have been murdered.

In June 1998 Carin Timo was watching ABC Television's *Australian Story*. It featured Ethnée as she promoted her autobiography, *Undaunted*. Ethnée explained her grief at the inexplicable disappearance of her second son. Carin watched, mouth agape. It was almost thirty years since Carin had last seen Simon and she never knew he had disappeared. When she heard this disturbing news the memories of her five months with Simon in the Carribean in 1970 came flooding back.

Ethnée travelled to Brisbane on a publicity tour, and Carin approached her at the book launch, eager to talk to her about Simon. After Ethnée had finished signing books, Carin walked up to Ethnée. 'Hello, Ethnée, my name is Carin. I used to know Simon.' Ethnée was shocked. While she always met people who said they knew her eldest son Robert, there were so few people who knew Simon.

At a later function for Ethnée, Carin saw Muche, who was also attending the event. They immediately recognised each other. They had both lived on Bribie Island, never realising they shared the unique connection: they were two long-lost friends of Simon Holmes à Court. They shared a history, intertwined but never intersecting. Carin worked at the local council offices on Bribie in the late seventies and had met Muche while processing development applications for him. Muche had settled there for a time, buying up petrol stations. It was a startling coincidence that two of them, who knew Simon so well from their time with him on opposite sides of the planet, should now be on each other's doorstep.

Gregg Lott is still sailing. After the adventure on the *Maggie May* he settled in Vanuatu for sixteen years before moving to a coastal town in New Zealand. He was last seen hitting the books, studying to attain a skipper's licence. He says the mystery of Simon's disappearance still 'sticks in my craw', with a husky drawl like he only left upstate New York yesterday. He says Simon was not the suicidal type.

The other crewman with Lott and Simon, Milton Skinner, now in his late seventies, lives in the coastal town of Mandurah, south of Perth.

Skinner lost contact with Simon but was coincidentally in

South Africa in 1977. Skinner was on holiday in October that year in the eastern Cape, just a month after Ethnée had been there searching for her son. On Ethnée's request Skinner also travelled to the Tsitsikamma forest to see the area for himself and met with Tim Liversedge in Johannesburg. Skinner came up with nothing. Skinner's only theory about Simon's disappearance was that he went hiking and was possibly bitten by a snake. 'He loved walking,' Skinner says. 'He bloody walked everywhere in the Seychelles.'

Skinner has remained good friends with Ethnée. He finds it difficult to believe that any kind of Cold War conspiracy contributed to Simon's death. But what of his missions up the East coast of Africa? Skinner was not aware of it but said he 'was a loner, definitely a loner. I think he was a pretty proud sort of bugger too, you know. Simon was not the sort of guy who would bother anybody and I don't think he would like to ask anyone for money. He was always keen to pay his way.'

Ron Wink, another of Simon's crew members on the *Maggie May*, lives in Perth. 'I am sure that by now you know one thing about him—that he was not "mainstream" in any way. He was a very private person. He kept his emotions, his thoughts and his feelings very much to himself. I often felt that Simon was a very "driven" person. He wanted to go places, achieve the photographic and sound recordings then move on. He just seemed to find it difficult to relax.'

Acknowledgments

This book wasn't much more than idea until the late John Iremonger of Allen & Unwin placed his faith in me. I only hope this would have, at the very least, met his expectations. Rebecca Kaiser took over the project at A&U and her enthusiasm, humour and gentle direction set me on the right path. Copy editor Jo Jarrah was fantastic at picking up on some continuity issues and thanks to Alex Nahlous for managing the editorial process and pulling the wonderful design elements to this book. Of course any errors or omissions remain mine.

From one publishing world to another: thanks to all my colleagues at News Limited and more specifically *The Australian* for the support and, on occasion, the time to finish *The Other Brother*; to editor Michael Stutchbury and editor-in-chief Chris Mitchell, and those formerly in that role, Campbell Reid and David Armstrong, respectively; to Clive Mathieson and my other colleagues and friends past and present on the business desk at *The Australian*—you all know who you are; and South African Michael Dorfling, who emigrated to Australia and arrived at *The Australian*, as far as I was concerned, at just the right time. His comments on my manuscript were invaluable. Also thanks to Ric Wilson, associate publisher, at Johnnic Communications in Port Elizabeth, who helped me source library archives for the newspaper clips that appear in the illustrative sections.

I made many friends around the world thanks to this book. Tim and June Liversedge have been an inspiration. Likewise Bodo and Robyn Muche. I also admired Daphne Hildebrandt's frankness in recounting her experiences. In Cape Town, Patrick Farrell has given great support over the years. Alide Dasnois gave me a job at *The Argus* back in 1995 and I would never have stumbled across this story if it wasn't for her. The clan in Cape Town who dubbed me 'Geoff the Bruce' also played a role in making my time in port city so special. And in Africa you would be hard pressed to find a better travelling companion than Dr Linda Harris.

Ethnée Holmes à Court is an amazing lady, eighty-nine years young. I spent many hours discussing her life and that of her sons on a number of occasions over the years. She holds such a sunny disposition despite the tragedy in her life; an inner strength to be admired and a compelling account of which can be found in her autobiography *Undaunted* (see 'Note on Sources'). Her grandson and Robert's son, Peter, also provided helpful advice. As a journalist I did not seek specific endorsement from the Holmes à Courts on this project but I hope they feel it serves the memory of Simon well.

To my family and my friends: thanks to one and all for the support, particularly my mother Else Hardy. Finally, and most importantly, to my wife Nikki: the completion of this book is another dream come true. The first was when I met her in Maun in 1996 with a grand plan to write a book. She believed in me. I thank her for her unfailing support and patience.

Note on Sources

The main sources for *The Other Brother* were interviews with the people who appear in the pages of this book, namely: Tim and June Liversedge; Bodo Muche; Ethnée Holmes à Court; Daphne Hildebrandt (nee Truter/Wilmot); Carin Timo; Gregg Lott; Milton Skinner; Ron Wink; David Kitching; Lorenda Savage; Lionel Palmer; Ronald Brooks; Hugh Roberton; Kent Ullberg; as well as dozens of Maun veterans like, among others, Ronnie Kayes, Anne Sanderburg and Joyce Bateman. I spoke with South African police from Storm's River and in Port Elizabeth, as well as experts in South Africa's counter intelligence years of the 1960s and 1970s.

This book also draws on periodical material from the state library in Port Elizabeth that helped set the scene in 1977 when Simon disappeared in the area, as well as the newspaper libraries of the *Evening Post* and the *Cape Argus* in Cape Town.

Books consulted include Ethnée Holmes à Court's autobiography *Undaunted* (Pan Macmillan, 1998) which was helpful as source material for the chapter 'The Early Days';

Mark and Delia Owens' *Cry of the Kalahari* (Houghton Mifflin Company, 1984); Patricia Edgar's biography *Janet Holmes à Court* (HarperCollinsPublishers, 1999); Norman Rush's *Mating* (First Vintage International, 1992); Nelson Mandela's *Long Walk to Freedom* (Abacus, 1994); Steve Biko's selected writings in *I Write What I Like* (The Bowerdean Press, 1978); *Africa*, edited by Phyllis M. Martin and Patrick O'Meara (Indiana University Press, 1995); Thomas Pakenham's *The Scramble for Africa* (Perennial, 1992); *Lonely Planet*'s *South Africa* (Lonely Planet Publications, 1993); *Lonely Planet*'s *Zimbabwe, Botswana & Namibia* (Lonely Planet Publications, 1995); Kenneth Newman's *Birds of Southern Africa* (HarperCollinsPublishers, 1988).